IM-TEPS

기출유형문제집

TEST

문제

IM-TEPS 기출유형문제집을 출간하며

에듀팡 어학연구소에서는 IM-TEPS 출제분석을 통해 1회분 실전문제를 담은 'IM-TEPS 기출유형문제집'을 출간하였습니다. IM-TEPS는 공인 영어능력 평가시험 TEPS를 성공적으로 수행해온 서울대학교 언어교육원에서 다년간의 연구를 통해 개발된 시험입니다. 중·고등학생에게 적합한 평가 방식을 통해 객관적이고, 정확한 언어능력 평가로 교육현장에서 중요한 학습의 기준을 제시할 것이라 기대됩니다.

IM-TEPS의 새로운 시작에 발맞춰 본 연구소에서는 IM-TEPS를 완벽하게 대비할 수 있도록 돕고자 본 문제집을 준비하였습니다. 실제와 유사한 듣기영역 평가와 출제 및 난이도 분석을 통한 최적화된 읽기영역 실전문제들로 구성하였습니다. 시험의 주요 대상인 중·고등학생의 특성을 고려하여, 어학능력뿐만 아니라 내신시험, 나아가 수능시험까지 대비할 수 있는 실용영어능력 향상을 위한 파트너가 되겠습니다.

최신 기출유형 문제 전격 공개

본 연구소에서는 IM-TEPS 출제 분석을 통해 선정된 문제 유형을 간추려 체계적으로 분류하여 IM-TEPS 기출유형 문제 1회분을 본 교재에 수록했습니다. 이를 통해 IM-TEPS 예비 수험생들은 새로이 치러지는 IM-TEPS 대비를 위해 문제의 유형과 특징을 학습할 수 있습니다. 실제 시험지와 동일한 시험 구성, 문제지 및 해설지 분권 구성, OMR 제공을 통해 실제와 가장 유사한 환경에서 IM-TEPS 시험 대비가 가능합니다.

실제 정기시험 성우 음성으로 대비

본 교재는 실제 정기 시험과 유사한 환경에서 듣기 영역 평가를 학습할 수 있도록 실제 시험과 동일한 성우로 녹음된 듣기영역 음원을 제공하고 있습니다. 제공된 음원을 통해 실전과 동일한 모의테스트가 가능하며, 시험 후 반복 학습으로 활용할 수 있습니다. 추가적인 학습을 위해 해설지 내 듣기 음원 해석본, 주요 어휘, Paraphrasing을 제공하여 듣기 실력향상을 위한 학습자료를 제공하고 있습니다.

핵심 포인트에 맞춘 명쾌한 해설

본 교재에서는 고득점을 위한 체계적인 문제 풀이 전략과 해설을 수록하였습니다. 출제분석을 통해 문제별 주제와 출제유형 및 난이도를 제공합니다. 문제의 주제에 대한 이해도를 높이고, 유형별 학습을 통해 취약한 문제를 파악하여 대비할 수 있습니다. 상세한 문제풀이와 문제 핵심포인트에 맞춘 출제분석, 주요 어휘학습을 통해 해설지만으로도 학습할 수 있습니다.

[IM-TEPS 기출유형문제집]을 통해 실용영어실력 향상과 함께 흔들리지 않는 영어 실력 확보로 IM-TEPS 목표 점수 도달뿐 아니라 이후 학습 여정에서 꾸준한 성과를 거두실 수 있기를 진심으로 응원합니다.

에듀팡 어학연구소

Contents

온라인 학습(www.imteps.com)

📱 IM-TEPS 듣기영역 MP3 음원

🖥 IM-TEPS 기출유형 문제 강의

이 책의 구성과 특징

01. IM-TEPS 최신 기출유형 문제 1회분 수록

듣기 영역

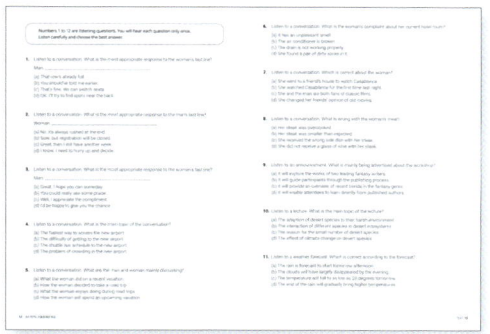

IM-TEPS 최신 출제 경향을 완벽 반영한 기출유형 문제 1회분을 정기시험 듣기영역의 실제 시험지 형태 그대로 구성했습니다.

실제 시험장에서 듣게 될 정기시험 성우 음성으로 실전 연습을 할 수 있도록 듣기영역 MP3 음원을 담았습니다.

읽기 영역

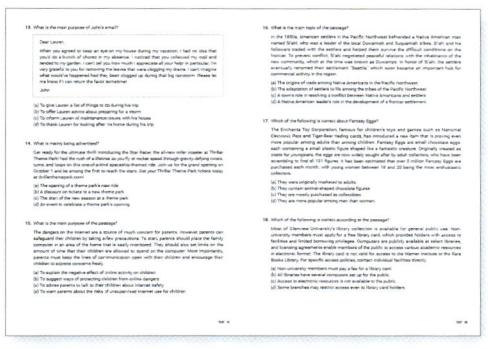

IM-TEPS 최신 출제 경향을 완벽 반영한 기출유형 문제 1회분을 정기시험 읽기영역의 실제 시험지 형태 그대로 구성했습니다.

OMR 답안지

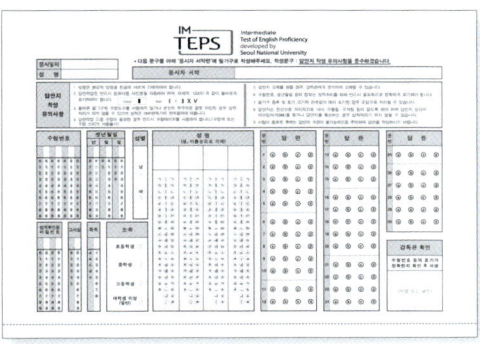

실제 시험장에서 사용하게 될 답안지로 실전 연습을 할 수 있도록 OMR 답안지를 담았습니다.

02. IM-TEPS 최신 기출유형 문제 정답 및 해설 수록

듣기 영역

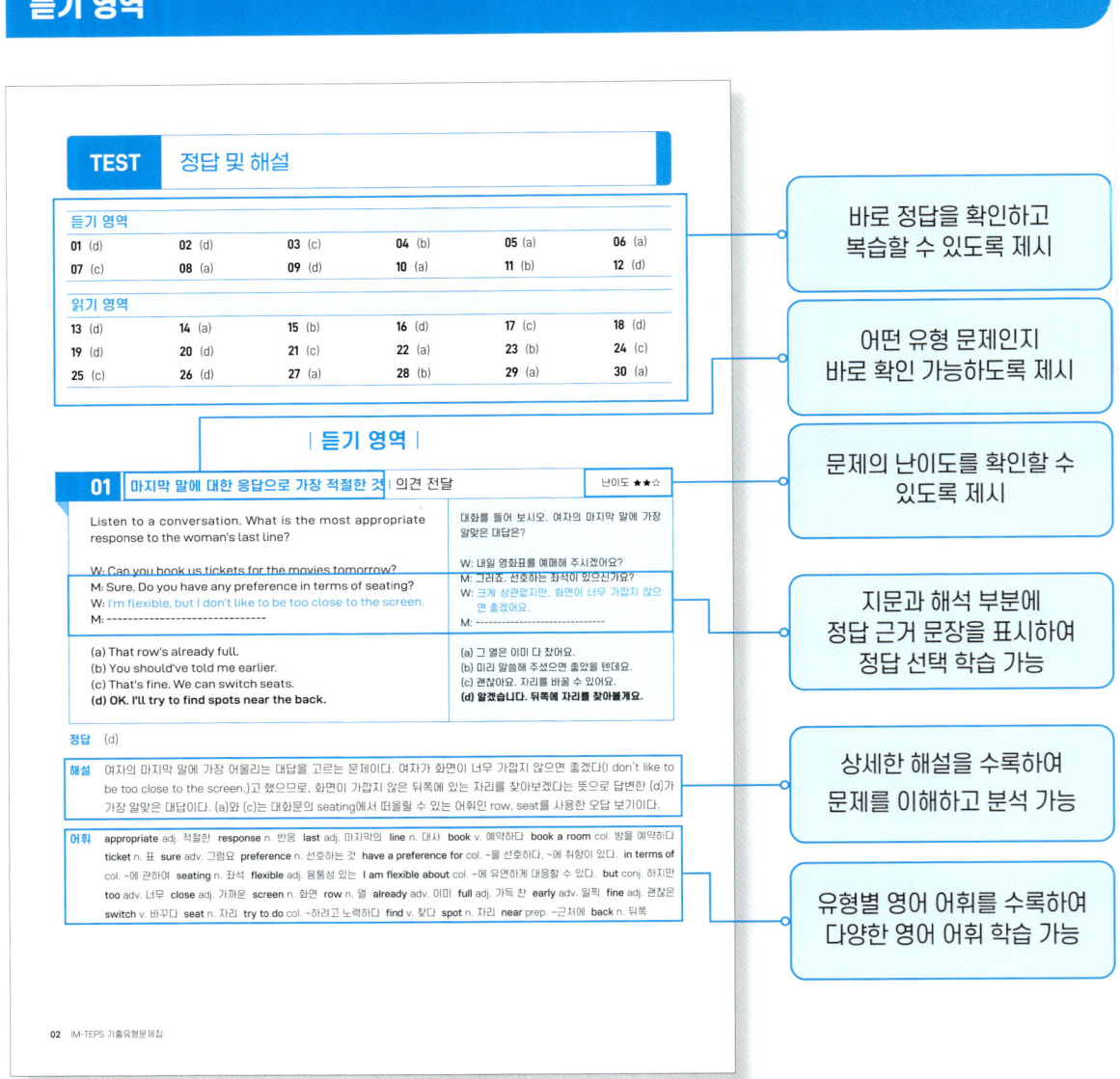

| TEST | 정답 및 해설 |

듣기 영역

| 01 (d) | 02 (d) | 03 (c) | 04 (b) | 05 (a) | 06 (a) |
| 07 (c) | 08 (a) | 09 (d) | 10 (a) | 11 (b) | 12 (d) |

읽기 영역

13 (d)	14 (a)	15 (b)	16 (d)	17 (c)	18 (d)
19 (d)	20 (d)	21 (c)	22 (b)	23 (b)	24 (c)
25 (c)	26 (d)	27 (c)	28 (b)	29 (a)	30 (a)

바로 정답을 확인하고 복습할 수 있도록 제시

어떤 유형 문제인지 바로 확인 가능하도록 제시

| 듣기 영역 |

01 | 마지막 말에 대한 응답으로 가장 적절한 것 | 의견 전달 | 난이도 ★★☆

문제의 난이도를 확인할 수 있도록 제시

Listen to a conversation. What is the most appropriate response to the woman's last line?

W: Can you book us tickets for the movies tomorrow?
M: Sure. Do you have any preference in terms of seating?
W: I'm flexible, but I don't like to be too close to the screen.
M: ------------------------------

(a) That row's already full.
(b) You should've told me earlier.
(c) That's fine. We can switch seats.
(d) OK. I'll try to find spots near the back.

대화를 들어 보시오. 여자의 마지막 말에 가장 알맞은 대답은?

W: 내일 영화표를 예매해 주시겠어요?
M: 그러죠. 선호하는 좌석이 있으신가요?
W: 크게 상관없지만, 화면이 너무 가깝지 않으면 좋겠어요.
M: ------------------------------

(a) 그 열은 이미 다 찼어요.
(b) 미리 말씀해 주셨으면 좋았을 텐데요.
(c) 괜찮아요. 자리를 바꿀 수 있어요.
(d) 알겠습니다. 뒤쪽에 자리를 찾아볼게요.

지문과 해석 부분에 정답 근거 문장을 표시하여 정답 선택 학습 가능

정답 (d)

해설 여자의 마지막 말에 가장 어울리는 대답을 고르는 문제이다. 여자가 화면이 너무 가깝지 않으면 좋겠다(I don't like to be too close to the screen.)고 했으므로, 화면이 가깝지 않은 뒤쪽에 있는 자리를 찾아보겠다는 뜻으로 답변한 (d)가 가장 알맞은 대답이다. (a)와 (c)는 대화문의 seating에서 떠올릴 수 있는 어휘인 row, seat을 사용한 오답 보기이다.

상세한 해설을 수록하여 문제를 이해하고 분석 가능

어휘 appropriate adj. 적절한 response n. 반응 last adj. 마지막의 line n. 대사 book v. 예약하다 book a room col. 방을 예약하다 ticket n. 표 sure adv. 그럼요 preference n. 선호하는 것 have a preference for col. ~을 선호하다, ~에 취향이 있다. in terms of col. ~에 관하여 seating n. 좌석 flexible adj. 융통성 있는 I am flexible about col. ~에 유연하게 대응할 수 있다. but conj. 하지만 too adv. 너무 close adj. 가까운 screen n. 화면 row n. 열 already adv. 이미 full adj. 가득 찬 early adv. 일찍 fine adj. 괜찮은 switch v. 바꾸다 seat n. 자리 try to do col. ~하려고 노력하다 find v. 찾다 spot n. 자리 near prep. ~근처에 back n. 뒤쪽

유형별 영어 어휘를 수록하여 다양한 영어 어휘 학습 가능

02 IM-TEPS 기출유형문제집

읽기 영역

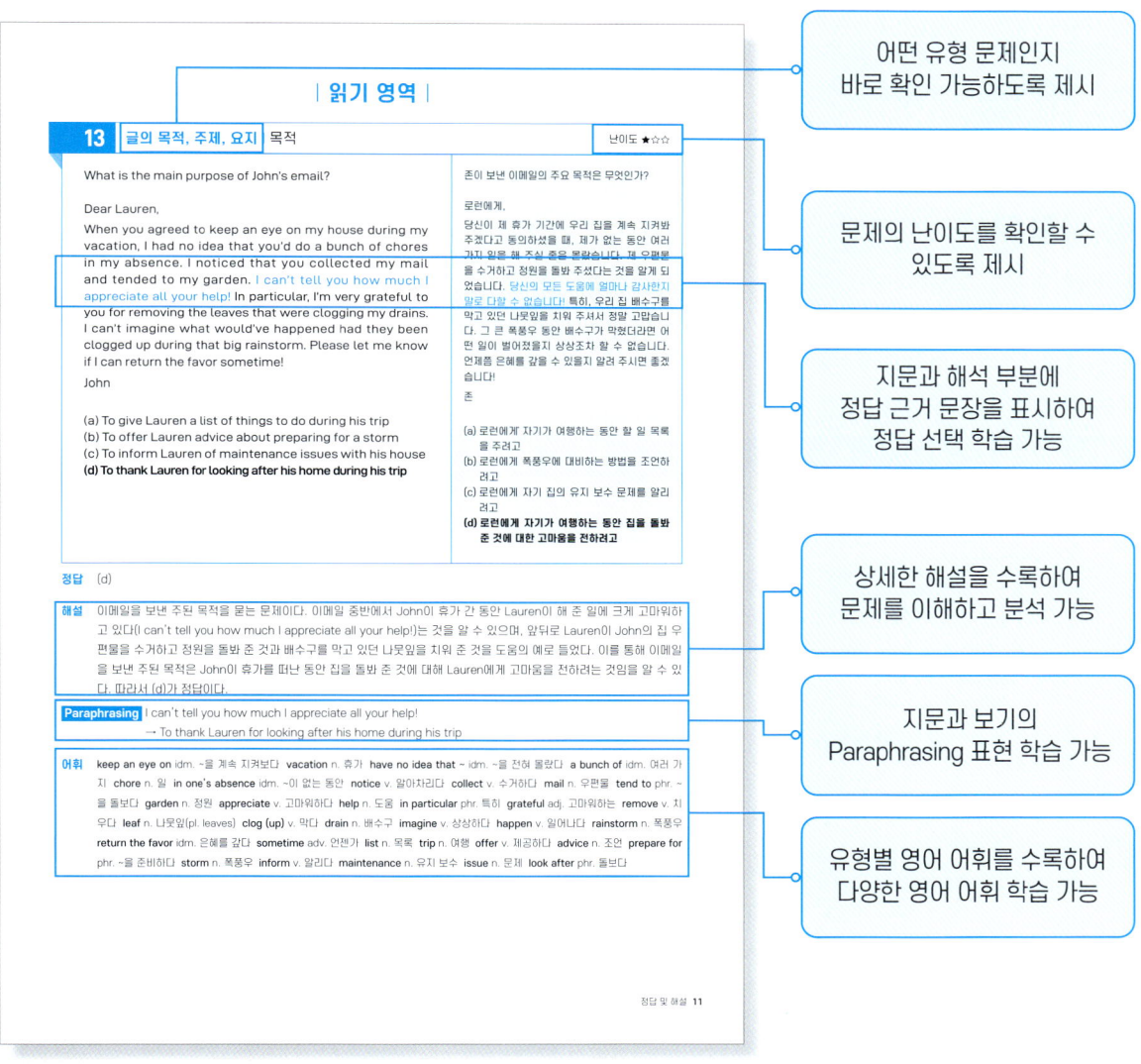

| 읽기 영역 |

13 글의 목적, 주제, 요지 | 목적
난이도 ★☆☆

What is the main purpose of John's email?

Dear Lauren,

When you agreed to keep an eye on my house during my vacation, I had no idea that you'd do a bunch of chores in my absence. I noticed that you collected my mail and tended to my garden. I can't tell you how much I appreciate all your help! In particular, I'm very grateful to you for removing the leaves that were clogging my drains. I can't imagine what would've happened had they been clogged up during that big rainstorm. Please let me know if I can return the favor sometime!

John

(a) To give Lauren a list of things to do during his trip
(b) To offer Lauren advice about preparing for a storm
(c) To inform Lauren of maintenance issues with his house
(d) To thank Lauren for looking after his home during his trip

존이 보낸 이메일의 주요 목적은 무엇인가?

로런에게,

당신이 제 휴가 기간에 우리 집을 계속 지켜봐 주겠다고 동의하셨을 때, 제가 없는 동안 여러 가지 일을 해 주실 줄은 몰랐습니다. 제 우편물을 수거하고 정원을 돌봐 주셨다는 것을 알게 되었습니다. 당신의 모든 도움에 얼마나 감사한지 말로 다할 수 없습니다! 특히, 우리 집 배수구를 막고 있던 나뭇잎을 치워 주셔서 정말 고맙습니다. 그 큰 폭풍우 동안 배수구가 막혔더라면 어떤 일이 벌어졌을지 상상조차 할 수 없습니다. 언제쯤 은혜를 갚을 수 있을지 알려 주시면 좋겠습니다!

존

(a) 로런에게 자기가 여행하는 동안 할 일 목록을 주려고
(b) 로런에게 폭풍우에 대비하는 방법을 조언하려고
(c) 로런에게 자기 집의 유지 보수 문제를 알리려고
(d) 로런에게 자기가 여행하는 동안 집을 돌봐 준 것에 대한 고마움을 전하려고

정답 (d)

해설 이메일을 보낸 주된 목적을 묻는 문제이다. 이메일 중반에서 John이 휴가 간 동안 Lauren이 해 준 일에 크게 고마워하고 있다(I can't tell you how much I appreciate all your help!)는 것을 알 수 있으며, 앞뒤로 Lauren이 John의 집 우편물을 수거하고 정원을 돌봐 준 것과 배수구를 막고 있던 나뭇잎을 치워 준 것을 도움의 예로 들었다. 이를 통해 이메일을 보낸 주된 목적은 John이 휴가를 떠난 동안 집을 돌봐 준 것에 대해 Lauren에게 고마움을 전하려는 것임을 알 수 있다. 따라서 (d)가 정답이다.

Paraphrasing I can't tell you how much I appreciate all your help!
→ To thank Lauren for looking after his home during his trip

어휘 keep an eye on idm. ~을 계속 지켜보다 vacation n. 휴가 have no idea that ~ idm. ~을 전혀 몰랐다 a bunch of idm. 여러 가지 chore n. 일 in one's absence idm. ~이 없는 동안 notice v. 알아차리다 collect v. 수거하다 mail n. 우편물 tend to phr. ~을 돌보다 garden n. 정원 appreciate v. 고마워하다 help n. 도움 in particular phr. 특히 grateful adj. 고마워하는 remove v. 치우다 leaf n. 나뭇잎(pl. leaves) clog (up) v. 막다 drain n. 배수구 imagine v. 상상하다 happen v. 일어나다 rainstorm n. 폭풍우 return the favor idm. 은혜를 갚다 sometime adv. 언젠가 list n. 목록 trip n. 여행 offer v. 제공하다 advice n. 조언 prepare for phr. ~을 준비하다 storm n. 폭풍우 inform v. 알리다 maintenance n. 유지 보수 issue n. 문제 look after phr. 돌보다

어떤 유형 문제인지
바로 확인 가능하도록 제시

문제의 난이도를 확인할 수
있도록 제시

지문과 해석 부분에
정답 근거 문장을 표시하여
정답 선택 학습 가능

상세한 해설을 수록하여
문제를 이해하고 분석 가능

지문과 보기의
Paraphrasing 표현 학습 가능

유형별 영어 어휘를 수록하여
다양한 영어 어휘 학습 가능

IM-TEPS 소개

ⓔ IM-TEPS란?

서울대가 만든 중·고등학생을 위한 영어능력 진단 평가

IM-TEPS는 서울대학교 언어교육원이 국가로부터 공식 인정받은 민간자격 국가공인 시험인 TEPS의 외국어능력평가 경험을 바탕으로 대한민국 중·고교생의 객관적인 영어능력 진단을 위한 평가도구로 개발된 시험입니다.

IM-TEPS는 Intermediate(중급)-TEPS의 약자로, 대한민국 중·고교생의 영어능력을 주기적으로 진단하여 후속 학습 활동에 유용한 피드백을 제공하고 학습동기를 고취하기 위한 시험입니다.

ⓔ 시험 구성

▶ 시험 대상 : 중등, 고등 전 학년
▶ 시험 시간 : 총 45분
▶ 문항 유형 : TEPS 유형 중 중·저 난이도 문항 유형으로 수능영어와 유사하게 구성
▶ 문항 형태 : 객관식 사지선다형

영역	문항 유형	문항 수	배점		수능 유형 비교
듣기	마지막 말에 대한 응답으로 가장 적절한 것	3문항	3점	36점	11-12번
	대화의 목적, 주제, 요지	2문항	3점		1-2번
	대화의 내용과 일치하는 것	3문항	3점		9번
	말의 목적, 주제, 요지	2문항	3점		1,16번
	말의 내용과 일치하는 것	2문항	3점		9번
읽기	글의 목적, 주제, 요지	4문항	3점	64점	18,20,22-24번
	글의 내용과 일치하는 것	4문항	3점		26-28번
	빈칸에 들어갈 말	4문항	4점		32-34번
	전체 흐름과 관계없는 문장	2문항	4점		35번
	글의 목적, 주제, 요지, 제목	2문항	4점		41번
	글의 내용과 일치하는 것		4점		45번
	글의 목적, 주제, 요지, 제목	2문항	4점		41번
	글의 내용과 일치하는 것		4점		45번
총 45분		**30문항**	**100점**		**-**

📝 시험 특징

▶ 서울대학교 언어교육원 TEPS 출제진 직접 출제
▶ 수능 영어 영역의 문항 유형을 반영하여 학습연장을 고려한 시험 출제
▶ 모든 문제 및 보기를 영문으로 구성하여 영어 시험에 대한 적응력을 높임
▶ 중·고등학생을 대상으로 응시집단 내 자기 수준 파악 가능

📝 평가 방식

▶ **평가요소**
  • 수능 영어 평가요소와 유사하게 영어의 4가지 영역 평가
    - 듣기는 원어민의 대화·담화를 듣고 이해하는 능력을 측정하고, 말하기는 불완전 대화·담화를 듣고 적절한 의사소통 기능을 적용하여
      이를 완성하는 능력을 간접적으로 측정
    - 읽기는 배경지식 및 글의 단서를 활용하여 의미를 이해하는 상호작용적 독해 능력을 측정하고, 쓰기는 글의 내용을 이해하고
      이를 문장으로 요약하거나 문단을 구성할 수 있는 능력을 간접적으로 측정

▶ **등급체계**
  • 수능 영어 등급체계와 유사한 9등급 체계

구분	1등급	2등급	3등급	4등급	5등급	6등급	7등급	8등급	9등급
IM-TEPS	90점 이상	80~89점	70~79점	60~69점	50~59점	40~49점	30~39점	20~29점	19점 이하
수능 영어	90점 이상	80~89점	70~79점	60~69점	50~59점	40~49점	30~39점	20~29점	19점 이하

📝 시험 접수 방법

▶ **정기시험 접수**
  • 개인접수 : IM-TEPS 접수사이트(www.imteps.or.kr) 에서 접수
  • 응 시 료 : 35,000원

▶ **기관 및 단체 특별시험 접수**
  • 특별시험 접수 및 문의
  • IM-TEPS 영업 대행사 에듀팡 홈페이지(www.edupang.com) / 고객센터 1644-1777

IM-TEPS

Intermediate Test of English Proficiency developed by
Seoul National University

1. Listen to a conversation. What is the most appropriate response to the woman's last line?

Man: _____

(a) That row's already full.
(b) You should've told me earlier.
(c) That's fine. We can switch seats.
(d) OK. I'll try to find spots near the back.

2. Listen to a conversation. What is the most appropriate response to the man's last line?

Woman: _____

(a) No, it's always rushed at the end.
(b) Sure, but registration will be closed.
(c) Great, then I still have another week.
(d) I know. I need to hurry up and decide.

3. Listen to a conversation. What is the most appropriate response to the woman's last line?

Man: _____

(a) Great. I hope you can someday.
(b) You could really use some praise.
(c) Well, I appreciate the compliment.
(d) I'd be happy to give you the chance.

4. Listen to a conversation. What is the main topic of the conversation?

(a) The fastest way to access the new airport
(b) The difficulty of getting to the new airport
(c) The shuttle bus schedule to the new airport
(d) The problem of crowding in the new airport

5. Listen to a conversation. What are the man and woman mainly discussing?

(a) What the woman did on a recent vacation
(b) How the woman decided to take a road trip
(c) What the woman enjoys doing during road trips
(d) How the woman will spend an upcoming vacation

6. Listen to a conversation. What is the woman's complaint about her current hotel room?

(a) It has an unpleasant smell.
(b) The air conditioner is broken.
(c) The drain is not working properly.
(d) She found a pair of dirty socks in it.

7. Listen to a conversation. Which is correct about the woman?

(a) She went to a friend's house to watch *Casablanca*.
(b) She watched *Casablanca* for the first time last night.
(c) She and the man are both fans of classic films.
(d) She changed her friends' opinion of old movies.

8. Listen to a conversation. What is wrong with the woman's meal?

(a) Her steak was overcooked.
(b) Her steak was smaller than expected.
(c) She received the wrong side dish with her steak.
(d) She did not receive a glass of wine with her steak.

9. Listen to an announcement. What is mainly being advertised about the workshop?

(a) It will explore the works of two leading fantasy writers.
(b) It will guide participants through the publishing process.
(c) It will provide an overview of recent trends in the fantasy genre.
(d) It will enable attendees to learn directly from published authors.

10. Listen to a lecture. What is the main topic of the lecture?

(a) The adaption of desert species to their harsh environment
(b) The interaction of different species in desert ecosystems
(c) The reason for the small number of desert species
(d) The effect of climate change on desert species

11. Listen to a weather forecast. Which is correct according to the forecast?

(a) The rain is forecast to start tomorrow afternoon.
(b) The clouds will have largely disappeared by the evening.
(c) The temperature will fall to as low as 23 degrees tomorrow.
(d) The end of the rain will gradually bring higher temperatures.

12. Listen to a talk. Which is correct according to the talk?

    (a) Adults prefer consistent eye contact during intellectual discussions.
    (b) Children are less likely than adults to maintain eye contact.
    (c) Avoiding eye contact does not help children on tasks.
    (d) Processing human faces is a mentally challenging task.

This is the end of the listening section. Please go on to number 13.

13. What is the main purpose of John's email?

> Dear Lauren,
>
> When you agreed to keep an eye on my house during my vacation, I had no idea that you'd do a bunch of chores in my absence. I noticed that you collected my mail and tended to my garden. I can't tell you how much I appreciate all your help! In particular, I'm very grateful to you for removing the leaves that were clogging my drains. I can't imagine what would've happened had they been clogged up during that big rainstorm. Please let me know if I can return the favor sometime!
>
> John

(a) To give Lauren a list of things to do during his trip
(b) To offer Lauren advice about preparing for a storm
(c) To inform Lauren of maintenance issues with his house
(d) To thank Lauren for looking after his home during his trip

14. What is mainly being advertised?

Get ready for the ultimate thrill! Introducing the Star Racer, the all-new roller coaster at Thriller Theme Park! Feel the rush of a lifetime as you fly at rocket speed through gravity-defying twists, turns, and loops on this one-of-a-kind spaceship-themed ride. Join us for the grand opening on October 1 and be among the first to reach the stars. Get your Thriller Theme Park tickets today at thrillerthemepark.com!

(a) The opening of a theme park's new ride
(b) A discount on tickets to a new theme park
(c) The start of the new season at a theme park
(d) An event to celebrate a theme park's opening

15. What is the main purpose of the passage?

The dangers on the Internet are a source of much concern for parents. However, parents can safeguard their children by taking a few precautions. To start, parents should place the family computer in an area of the home that is easily monitored. They should also set limits on the amount of time that their children are allowed to spend on the computer. Most importantly, parents must keep the lines of communication open with their children and encourage their children to express concerns freely.

(a) To explain the negative effect of online activity on children
(b) To suggest ways of protecting children from online dangers
(c) To advise parents to talk to their children about Internet safety
(d) To warn parents about the risks of unsupervised Internet use for children

16. What is the main topic of the passage?

In the 1850s, American settlers in the Pacific Northwest befriended a Native American man named Si'ahl, who was a leader of the local Duwamish and Suquamish tribes. Si'ahl and his followers traded with the settlers and helped them survive the difficult conditions on the frontier. To prevent conflict, Si'ahl negotiated peaceful relations with the inhabitants of the new community, which at the time was known as Duwamps. In honor of Si'ahl, the settlers eventually renamed their settlement "Seattle," which soon became an important hub for commercial activity in the region.

(a) The origins of trade among Native Americans in the Pacific Northwest
(b) The adaptation of settlers to life among the tribes of the Pacific Northwest
(c) A town's role in resolving a conflict between Native Americans and settlers
(d) A Native American leader's role in the development of a frontier settlement

17. Which of the following is correct about Fantasy Eggs?

The Enchanta Toy Corporation, famous for children's toys and games such as Nanomal Electronic Pets and Tiger-Bear trading cards, has introduced a new item that is proving even more popular among adults than among children. Fantasy Eggs are small chocolate eggs, each containing a small plastic figure shaped like a fantastic creature. Originally created as treats for youngsters, the eggs are now widely sought after by adult collectors, who have been scrambling to find all 131 figures. It has been estimated that over 5 million Fantasy Eggs are purchased each month, with young women between 18 and 20 being the most enthusiastic collectors.

(a) They were originally marketed to adults.
(b) They contain animal-shaped chocolate figures.
(c) They are mostly purchased as collectibles.
(d) They are more popular among men than women.

18. Which of the following is correct according to the passage?

Most of Glenview University's library collection is available for general public use. Non-university members must apply for a free library card, which provides holders with access to facilities and limited borrowing privileges. Computers are publicly available at select libraries, and licensing agreements enable members of the public to access various academic resources in electronic format. The library card is not valid for access to the Warner Institute or the Rare Books Library. For specific access policies, contact individual facilities directly.

(a) Non-university members must pay a fee for a library card.
(b) All libraries have several computers set up for the public.
(c) Access to electronic resources is not available to the public.
(d) Some branches may restrict access even to library card holders.

19. Which of the following is correct according to the announcement?

Attention Skyline Condo Residents. As part of our regular activities, Building Management will be conducting a routine maintenance check next week. An inspection team will visit apartments between 9:30 a.m. and 4 p.m. on April 12 and 13. Door locks, window locks, motion sensors, and fire detectors will be checked, and repairs will be carried out as needed at residents' expense. If you will not be home during the inspection period, the inspection team will not be able to check your property. If you would like to schedule an inspection at another time, please contact Building Management to arrange one that is suitable for you.

(a) All maintenance checks will be conducted on the same day.
(b) The cost of repairs will be covered by Building Management.
(c) The inspection team will enter homes during residents' absence.
(d) Residents may set up a maintenance check at alternative times.

20. According to the passage, which animal has a higher brain-size-to-body-size ratio than humans?

Brain size is not considered an indicator of the intelligence of animal species. Large-brained species—the sperm whale being the creature with the largest brain of all—tend to have very large bodies. A more reliable measure of intelligence is actually the ratio of brain size to body size. Humans have the second highest ratio of brain-size to body-size of all living creatures, followed by porpoises. Many other highly intelligent creatures—including elephants—also score highly on this metric. However, this ratio is not a perfect indicator of intelligence, either. The highest-scoring creature on this metric is the tree shrew, which comes out cn top more because of its small body than because of its large brain.

(a) Sperm whales
(b) Porpoises
(c) Elephants
(d) Tree shrews

[21–24] Choose the option that is most appropriate to fill in the gaps below.

21. Watercolor painting has acquired a reputation as an amateur pastime. However, it _____ _____. In fact, many renowned artists, from the Renaissance to modern times, have used watercolor as a major medium for their works, including John Singer Sargent, Edward Hopper, and Georgia O'Keeffe. That such prestigious artists have devoted themselves to watercolor disproves the notion that the medium is simply for hobbyists and not for serious professionals.

(a) has yet to become popular in the art market
(b) is a favored medium of several lesser-known artists
(c) is actually an integral part of a long artistic tradition
(d) has recently lost its popularity among amateur artists

22. Third Culture Kids (TCKs)—children who grow up outside of their home countries because their parents are working or living overseas—generally _____. Due to this fact, they often think of themselves as belonging to a distinct community, one based on a shared experience of coming of age between distinct national cultures. Unfortunately, even after returning to their home countries, many feel like the only people who truly relate to them are fellow TCKs, as they continue to feel like outsiders not only in foreign countries but also in their countries of origin.

(a) find it easier to relate to each other than to non-TCKs
(b) discover that they adapt easily to unfamiliar cultures
(c) struggle to identify with their parents' generation
(d) grow up to become successful global citizens

23. In 1935, US scientists conducted a groundbreaking study on the effect of diet. The scientists fed rats a diet that was very low in calories but that contained all the necessary nutrients for normal development. These rats were then compared with rats that were fed normally. The scientists discovered that _____. The study has been replicated numerous times with a range of different animal species, with the results showing each time that a low-calorie diet leads to an extended lifespan and a lower risk of contracting diseases. Scientists theorize that limiting calorie intake is beneficial because it slows certain metabolic processes that result in oxidative damage to cells.

(a) normal growth requires sufficient calories and nutrients
(b) the former group lived significantly longer and healthier lives
(c) nutrient deficiencies are the leading cause of abnormal growth
(d) low-calorie diets do not necessarily result in nutrient deficiencies

24. In the 18th century, the French philosopher and writer Jean-Jacques Rousseau proposed a radically new view of human nature. In contrast to medieval European scholars, who tended to view humans as wicked by nature, Rousseau argued that humans were inherently peaceful and altruistic. According to Rousseau, humans' essential goodness had simply been corrupted by the negative influence of human civilization. This view represented a break with centuries of European religious tradition, which had placed the blame for moral corruption on the effects of original sin. On the basis of his views, Rousseau insisted that it was necessary to _____ _____.

(a) suppress the naturally wicked tendencies of most individuals
(b) modernize the teaching of religion for the betterment of society
(c) reform society in order to preserve the natural goodness of individuals
(d) return to more traditional ways of teaching people about right and wrong

25. Which of the following sentences does NOT fit in the overall flow of the passage?

The typical layout of a Japanese office can be seen as a reflection of the traditional values of Japanese society. (a) Unlike American offices, which often feature individual cubicles, Japanese offices tend to have open-plan layouts. (b) Such a layout encourages collaboration, reflecting the Japanese emphasis on collective rather than individual effort. (c) Nonetheless, Japanese employees who take time off work or come in late are sometimes seen as betraying their coworkers. (d) At the same time, the open-plan layout facilitates close employee supervision, which is important in Japan's hierarchical society.

26. Which of the following sentences does NOT fit in the overall flow of the passage?

A number of factors have contributed to the growing popularity of plastic surgery in recent years. (a) Advancements in medical technology have improved the safety and effectiveness of procedures, in addition to reducing recovery times. (b) On top of that, the growing influence of social media, combined with celebrity culture, has driven many people to pursue perceived beauty standards. (c) Society has also simply become more accepting of plastic surgery, reducing the stigma associated with undergoing procedures purely for aesthetic purposes. (d) While plastic surgery offers numerous benefits, it is important for anyone contemplating undergoing a cosmetic procedure to have realistic expectations.

[27-28] Read the following passage and answer the questions.

In 1972, sociologist Stanley Cohen introduced the concept of moral panics. He defined these events as widespread outbreaks of fear, anger, or outrage stemming from the perception that some specific behavior, group, or phenomenon poses a significant threat to the well-being of society. Some moral panics arise from actual threats, while others arise from purely imaginary ones. Regardless of whether the threat is real or imaginary, the extent of the danger to society is grossly exaggerated by the people caught up in the moral panic. Since Cohen's time, the concept of moral panics has been used to explain a number of significant historical events. For example, the McCarthy era in the United States has been characterized as a moral panic. During this period, from the late 1940s to the mid-1950s, US senator Joseph McCarthy whipped up public hysteria about the supposed influence of communism and Soviet agents on American institutions. As a result of the panic, thousands of innocent Americans were investigated by the Federal Bureau of Investigation (FBI) and blacklisted from participating in the entertainment industry. Another example is the War on Drugs, which reached its peak in the 1990s. During this period of US history, society became obsessed with the supposed threat of drugs. Due to these exaggerated fears, harsh laws were passed, resulting in many people being handed long prison sentences for relatively minor offenses.

27. What is the best title for the passage?

(a) The Concept of Moral Panics: Definition and Examples
(b) Updating the Definition of Moral Panics: Latest Discoveries
(c) Moral Panics: How They Have Changed throughout History
(d) The Effects of Moral Panics: Examples from around the World

28. Which of the following is correct according to the passage?

(a) Cohen expanded upon the existing theory of moral panics in 1972.
(b) Moral panics arise in response to both imaginary and real dangers.
(c) McCarthy warned the public about threats to communism.
(d) The US War on Drugs reached its highest point before 1990.

[29-30] Read the following passage and answer the questions.

The Playboy of the Western World, a three-act play by Irish playwright J. M. Synge, presented a strikingly original portrayal of the common people of Ireland. The play premiered in 1907 at Dublin's Abbey Theater, the national theater and one of Ireland's leading cultural institutions. At the time, Ireland remained firmly under control of the English, who had tended to depict the Irish as boorish subordinates. In opposition to these unflattering portraits, Irish nationalist writers had depicted poor Irish characters in often highly romantic terms, transforming these characters into symbols of national pride. Synge, who was fiercely nationalistic himself, saw the danger of such portraits, arguing that they were just as misrepresentative of the actual people as the insulting depictions by English writers. He wanted to present a true-to-life portrait, so instead of showing characters valiantly suffering under the burden of poverty, he depicted them often reveling in the crude humor and cheerful immorality of their surroundings. Unsurprisingly, his play was attacked by many of his own people, with the audience at the premiere going so far as to riot.

29. What is the main idea of the passage?

(a) Synge's uncommonly realistic depiction of Irish people caused controversy.
(b) Synge promoted nationalism in response to English depictions of the Irish.
(c) Synge was critical of inaccurate depiction of the Irish by English authors.
(d) Synge's blend of nationalism and romanticism divided Irish audiences.

30. Which of the following is correct according to the passage?

(a) The play was initially performed at a highly reputable theater.
(b) Synge wrote the play following Ireland's independence from England.
(c) Irish nationalist writers tended to avoid depicting lower-class Irish characters.
(d) Synge's play was celebrated upon its premiere but subsequently attracted harsh criticism.

Check whether you have correctly written and marked the necessary information on your answer sheet.

IM-TEPS

Intermediate Test of English Proficiency developed by
Seoul National University

IM-TEPS

Intermediate
Test of English Proficiency
developed by
Seoul National University

• 다음 문구를 아래 '응시자 서약란'에 필기구로 작성해주세요. 작성문구 : 답안지 작성 유의사항을 준수하겠습니다.

응시자 서약

응시일자

성명

답안지 작성 유의사항

1. 성명은 본인의 성명을 한글로 바르게 기재하여야 합니다.
2. 답안작성은 반드시 컴퓨터용 사인펜을 사용해야 하며, 아래의 'GOOD'과 같이 올바르게 표기하여야 합니다.

Good	Bad
●	⦿ ◗ ⊘ ✓

3. 올바른 필기구를 사용하지 않거나 본인의 부주의로 잘못 마킹한 경우 성적 처리가 되지 않을 수 있으므로 OMR판독기의 판독결과에 따릅니다.
4. 답안작성 도중 수정이 필요한 경우 반드시 수정테이프를 사용해야 합니다.(수정액 또는 수정 스티커 사용불가)

5. 답안지 교체를 원할 경우, 감독관에게 문의하여 교체할 수 있습니다.
6. 수험번호, 성명(성)등의 정보는 석차처리를 위해 반드시 정확하게 표기해야 합니다.
7. 필기구 종류 및 표기 크기와 관계없이 예비 표기한 경우 오답으로 처리될 수 있습니다.
8. 답안지는 전산으로 처리되므로 낙서, 이물질, 구겨짐 등이 없도록 해야 답안지 신원 타임마크(III)를 찢거나 답안지를 훼손하는 경우 석차처리가 되지 않을 수 있습니다.
9. 시험이 종료된 후에는 답안의 수정이 불가능하므로 주의하여 답안을 작성하시기 바랍니다.

수험번호

0 1 2 3 4 5 6 7 8 9
0 1 2 3 4 5 6 7 8 9
0 1 2 3 4 5 6 7 8 9
0 1 2 3 4 5 6 7 8 9
0 1 2 3 4 5 6 7 8 9

성적확인용 비밀번호

0 1 2 3 4 5 6 7 8 9
0 1 2 3 4 5 6 7 8 9
0 1 2 3 4 5 6 7 8 9
0 1 2 3 4 5 6 7 8 9

고사실

0 1 2 3 4 5
0 1 2 3 4 5

좌석

1 2 3 4 5 6 7 8
a b c d e f g h

생년월일

년	월	일
0 1 2 3 4 5 6 7 8 9	0 1	0 1 2 3

성별

남 □ 여 □

소속

초등학생 ○
중학생 ○
고등학생 ○
대학생 이상 (일반) ○

성 명 (성, 이름순으로 기재)

(한글 자모 표기란)

답 란

문번	답 란
1	a b c d
2	a b c d
3	a b c d
4	a b c d
5	a b c d
6	a b c d
7	a b c d
8	a b c d
9	a b c d
10	a b c d
11	a b c d
12	a b c d

문번	답 란
13	a b c d
14	a b c d
15	a b c d
16	a b c d
17	a b c d
18	a b c d
19	a b c d
20	a b c d
21	a b c d
22	a b c d
23	a b c d
24	a b c d

문번	답 란
25	a b c d
26	a b c d
27	a b c d
28	a b c d
29	a b c d
30	a b c d

감독관 확인

수험번호 등의 표기가 정확한지 확인 후 서명

(서명 또는 날인)

IM TEPS

Intermediate
Test of English Proficiency
developed by
Seoul National University

• 다음 문구를 아래 '응시자 서약란'에 필기구로 작성해주세요. 작성문구 : 답안지 작성 유의사항을 준수하겠습니다.

응시자 서약

응시일자	
성 명	

답안지 작성 유의사항

1. 성명은 본인의 성명을 한글로 바르게 기재하여야 합니다.
2. 답안작성은 반드시 컴퓨터용 사인펜을 사용해야 하며, 아래의 'GOOD' 과 같이 올바르게 표기하여야 합니다.

   Good ● Bad ⊙ ◑ ⊗ Ⓧ ✓

3. 올바른 필기구와 수정도구를 사용하지 않거나 본인의 부주의로 잘못된 경우 성적 처리가 되지 않을 수 있으며 성적은 OMR판독기에 판독결과에 따릅니다.
4. 답안지는 도중 수정이 필요한 경우 반드시 수정테이프를 사용해야 합니다.(수정액이 또는 수정용 스티커 사용불가)

5. 답안지 교체를 원할 경우, 감독관에게 문의하여 교체할 수 있습니다.
6. 수험번호, 생년월일 등의 정보는 성적처리를 위해 반드시 필요하므로 정확하게 표기해야 합니다.
7. 필기구 종류 및 표기 크기/관계없이 예비 표기한 경우 오답으로 처리될 수 있습니다.
8. 답안지는 접선으로 처리되므로 낙서, 이물질 등이 구겨진 경우 성적처리가 되지 않을 수 있습니다.
9. 시험이 종료된 후에는 답안의 수정이 불가능하므로 주의하여 답안을 작성하시기 바랍니다.

성별	
남 ◯	여 ◯

소속
초등학생 ◯
중학생 ◯
고등학생 ◯
대학생 이상 (일반) ◯

성 명
(성, 이름순으로 기재)

문번	답란				문번	답란				문번	답란			
1	ⓐ	ⓑ	ⓒ	ⓓ	13	ⓐ	ⓑ	ⓒ	ⓓ	25	ⓐ	ⓑ	ⓒ	ⓓ
2	ⓐ	ⓑ	ⓒ	ⓓ	14	ⓐ	ⓑ	ⓒ	ⓓ	26	ⓐ	ⓑ	ⓒ	ⓓ
3	ⓐ	ⓑ	ⓒ	ⓓ	15	ⓐ	ⓑ	ⓒ	ⓓ	27	ⓐ	ⓑ	ⓒ	ⓓ
4	ⓐ	ⓑ	ⓒ	ⓓ	16	ⓐ	ⓑ	ⓒ	ⓓ	28	ⓐ	ⓑ	ⓒ	ⓓ
5	ⓐ	ⓑ	ⓒ	ⓓ	17	ⓐ	ⓑ	ⓒ	ⓓ	29	ⓐ	ⓑ	ⓒ	ⓓ
6	ⓐ	ⓑ	ⓒ	ⓓ	18	ⓐ	ⓑ	ⓒ	ⓓ	30	ⓐ	ⓑ	ⓒ	ⓓ
7	ⓐ	ⓑ	ⓒ	ⓓ	19	ⓐ	ⓑ	ⓒ	ⓓ					
8	ⓐ	ⓑ	ⓒ	ⓓ	20	ⓐ	ⓑ	ⓒ	ⓓ					
9	ⓐ	ⓑ	ⓒ	ⓓ	21	ⓐ	ⓑ	ⓒ	ⓓ					
10	ⓐ	ⓑ	ⓒ	ⓓ	22	ⓐ	ⓑ	ⓒ	ⓓ					
11	ⓐ	ⓑ	ⓒ	ⓓ	23	ⓐ	ⓑ	ⓒ	ⓓ					
12	ⓐ	ⓑ	ⓒ	ⓓ	24	ⓐ	ⓑ	ⓒ	ⓓ					

수험번호

성적확인용 비밀번호

고사실

좌석

생년월일
년 월 일

감독관 확인
수험번호 등의 표기가 정확한지 확인 후 서명
(서명 또는 날인)

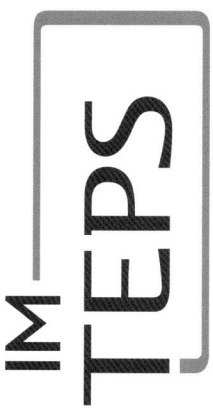

IM-TEPS 기출유형문제집 1회분

발행일	2024년 7월 31일
지은이	에듀팡 어학연구소 편집·해설
펴낸이	애듀팡 출판팀
펴낸곳	에듀팡
주소	서울특별시 구로구 디지털로 306 대륭포스트타워 2차 612호
홈페이지	www.edupang.com
고객센터	1644-1777
출판등록	2024년 7월 11일 제25100-2024-000041호
ISBN	979-11-988484-1-3 53740

MEMO

IM-TEPS
기출유형문제집

TEST
정답 및 해설

듣기 영역

01 (d)	**02** (d)	**03** (c)	**04** (b)	**05** (a)	**06** (a)
07 (c)	**08** (a)	**09** (d)	**10** (a)	**11** (b)	**12** (d)

읽기 영역

13 (d)	**14** (a)	**15** (b)	**16** (d)	**17** (c)	**18** (d)
19 (d)	**20** (d)	**21** (c)	**22** (a)	**23** (b)	**24** (c)
25 (c)	**26** (d)	**27** (a)	**28** (b)	**29** (a)	**30** (a)

| 듣기 영역 |

01 마지막 말에 대한 응답으로 가장 적절한 것 | 의견 전달   난이도 ★★☆

Listen to a conversation. What is the most appropriate response to the woman's last line?

W: Can you book us tickets for the movies tomorrow?
M: Sure. Do you have any preference in terms of seating?
W: I'm flexible, but I don't like to be too close to the screen.
M: ---------------------------

(a) That row's already full.
(b) You should've told me earlier.
(c) That's fine. We can switch seats.
(d) OK. I'll try to find spots near the back.

대화를 들어 보시오. 여자의 마지막 말에 가장 알맞은 대답은?

W: 내일 영화표를 예매해 주시겠어요?
M: 그러죠. 선호하는 좌석이 있으신가요?
W: 크게 상관없지만, 화면이 너무 가깝지 않으면 좋겠어요.
M: ---------------------------

(a) 그 열은 이미 다 찼어요.
(b) 미리 말씀해 주셨으면 좋았을 텐데요.
(c) 괜찮아요. 자리를 바꿀 수 있어요.
(d) 알겠습니다. 뒤쪽에 자리를 찾아볼게요.

정답 (d)

해설 여자의 마지막 말에 가장 어울리는 대답을 고르는 문제이다. 여자가 화면이 너무 가깝지 않으면 좋겠다(I don't like to be too close to the screen.)고 했으므로, 화면이 가깝지 않은 뒤쪽에 있는 자리를 찾아보겠다는 뜻으로 답변한 (d)가 가장 알맞은 대답이다. (a)와 (c)는 대화문의 seating에서 떠올릴 수 있는 어휘인 row, seat를 사용한 오답 보기이다.

어휘 appropriate adj. 적절한 response n. 반응 last adj. 마지막의 line n. 대사 book v. 예약하다 book a room col. 방을 예약하다 ticket n. 표 sure adv. 그럼요 preference n. 선호하는 것 have a preference for col. ~을 선호하다, ~에 취향이 있다. in terms of col. ~에 관하여 seating n. 좌석 flexible adj. 융통성 있는 I am flexible about col. ~에 유연하게 대응할 수 있다. but conj. 하지만 too adv. 너무 close adj. 가까운 screen n. 화면 row n. 열 already adv. 이미 full adj. 가득 찬 early adv. 일찍 fine adj. 괜찮은 switch v. 바꾸다 seat n. 자리 try to do col. ~하려고 노력하다 find v. 찾다 spot n. 자리 near prep. ~근처에 back n. 뒤쪽

02 마지막 말에 대한 응답으로 가장 적절한 것 | 정보 전달

난이도 ★★☆

Listen to a conversation. What is the most appropriate response to the man's last line?

M: Have you signed up for classes yet?
W: Not yet. I'm still debating what to take.
M: But the registration deadline is tomorrow.
W: ---------------------------

(a) No, it's always rushed at the end.
(b) Sure, but registration will be closed.
(c) Great, then I still have another week.
(d) I know. I need to hurry up and decide.

대화를 들어보시오. 남자의 마지막 말에 가장 알맞은 대답은?

M: 수강 신청 하셨나요?
W: 아직이요. 아직 어떤 강좌를 들을지 고민하고 있어요.
M: 하지만 등록 마감일이 내일이에요.
W: ---------------------------

(a) 아니요, 항상 마지막에 등록을 서두르게 돼요.
(b) 그래요, 하지만 등록은 마감될 거예요.
(c) 좋아요, 그럼 아직 한 주 더 있네요.
(d) 알아요. 서둘러 결정해야 해요.

정답 (d)

해설 남자의 마지막 말에 가장 어울리는 대답을 고르는 문제이다. 남자가 등록 마감일이 내일이라고 했으므로, 서둘러 결정해야 한다고 답변한 (d)가 가장 알맞은 대답이다. (b)는 대화문의 registration을, (c)는 still을 반복해 의미 혼동을 유도한 오답 보기이다.

어휘 sign up for phr. ~을 신청하다 class n. 강좌 debate v. 토론하다, 숙고하다 take v. 수강하다 registration n. 등록 deadline n. 마감일 rush v. 서두르다 at the end idm. 마지막에 sure adv. 그래요 close v. 마감하다 then adv. 그러면 need to aux. ~해야 한다 hurry up phr. 서두르다 decide v. 결정하다

03 마지막 말에 대한 응답으로 가장 적절한 것 | 의견 전달

난이도 ★☆☆

Listen to a conversation. What is the most appropriate response to the woman's last line?

W: Your band put on a great show tonight.
M: Thanks. I think we've had better performances, though.
W: Your shows are always good, but this one really stood out to me.
M: ---------------------------

(a) Great. I hope you can someday.
(b) You could really use some praise.
(c) Well, I appreciate the compliment.
(d) I'd be happy to give you the chance.

대화를 들어 보시오. 여자의 마지막 말에 가장 알맞은 대답은?

W: 당신 밴드가 오늘 밤에 훌륭한 공연을 했어요.
M: 고맙습니다. 하지만 우리는 과거에 더 나은 공연을 했던 적이 있었던 것 같아요.
W: 당신 밴드의 공연은 항상 좋지만, 제가 보기에 이번 공연은 정말 빼어났어요.
M: ---------------------------

(a) 좋아요. 언젠가 그럴 수 있기를 바랍니다.
(b) 정말로 칭찬받을 만하세요.
(c) 그래요, 칭찬해 주셔서 고맙습니다.
(d) 기회를 드리게 된다면 기쁠 텐데요.

정답 (c)

해설 여자의 마지막 말에 가장 어울리는 대답을 고르는 문제이다. 여자가 이번 공연이 정말 빼어났다고 했으므로, 칭찬해 주어서 고맙다고 한 (c)가 가장 알맞은 대답이다.

어휘 band n. 밴드 put on a show idm. 공연하다 performance n. 공연 though adv. 하지만 but conj. 하지만 stand out phr. 빼어나다 hope v. 바라다 someday adv. 언젠가 praise n. 칭찬 appreciate v. 감사하다 compliment n. 칭찬 chance n. 기회 be happy to phr. 기꺼이 ~하다

Listen to a conversation. What is the main topic of the conversation?

W: The new airport is really spacious and modern.
M: True. But getting there is a nightmare.
W: It is rather far from the city center.
M: Plus, there's so much traffic, and parking is awful.
W: Isn't there a shuttle service directly there?
M: There is, but the buses don't run that frequently.
W: It would be helpful if there were a rail link.

(a) The fastest way to access the new airport
(b) The difficulty of getting to the new airport
(c) The shuttle bus schedule to the new airport
(d) The problem of crowding in the new airport

대화를 들어 보시오. 대화의 주제는 무엇인가?

W: 새 공항은 정말 넓고 현대적이에요.
M: 맞아요. 하지만 거기에 가는 일은 악몽 같아요.
W: 도시 중심부에서는 상당히 멀어요.
M: 게다가 교통량이 많고, 주차도 끔찍해요.
W: 곧장 가는 셔틀 서비스가 있지 않나요?
M: 있긴 한데, 버스가 그렇게 자주 다니지는 않아요.
W: 철도가 연결되어 있다면 도움이 될 텐데요.

(a) 새 공항에 가장 빠르게 접근하는 방법
(b) 새 공항에 가는 것의 어려움
(c) 새 공항으로 가는 셔틀버스 운행 시간표
(d) 새 공항의 혼잡 문제

정답 (b)

해설 대화의 주제를 묻는 문제이다. 여자가 새로 생긴 공항을 화제로 꺼내자, 화자들은 도시 중심부에서 멀고(It is rather far from the city center.) 교통량이 많으며 주차도 불편해서(Plus, there's so much traffic, and parking is awful.) 새 공항에 가기가 어렵다는 데 동의했다. 따라서 (b)가 정답이다.

어휘 main adj. 주요한 topic n. 주제 spacious adj. 넓은 modern adj. 현대적인 true adj. 맞는 get v. 가다 nightmare n. 악몽 rather adv. 상당히 far adj. 멀리 떨어진 city n. 도시 center n. 중심 plus conj. 게다가 traffic n. 교통량 parking n. 주차 awful adj. 끔찍한 shuttle n. 셔틀 service n. 서비스 directly adv. 곧장 frequently adv. 자주 helpful adj. 도움이 되는 rail n. 철도 link n. 연결 fast adj. 빠른 way n. 방법 access v. 접근하다 shuttle bus n. 셔틀버스 schedule n. 시간표 problem n. 문제 crowding n. 혼잡

Listen to a conversation. What are the man and woman mainly discussing?

M: Diana, you're back! How was your vacation?
W: Amazing! I spent two weeks driving cross-country.
M: Really? You must have covered a lot of ground.
W: Yeah, I saw some great natural scenery along the way.
M: Did you stop at many interesting places?
W: Of course. There were some great towns along the route.

(a) What the woman did on a recent vacation
(b) How the woman decided to take a road trip
(c) What the woman enjoys doing during road trips
(d) How the woman will spend an upcoming vacation

대화를 들어 보시오. 남자와 여자가 주로 이야기하고 있는 것은?

M: 다이애나, 돌아왔구나! 휴가는 어땠어?
W: 정말 좋았어! 2주 동안 차를 몰고 전국을 다녔어.
M: 정말이야? 정말 많은 곳을 돌아다녔겠다.
W: 그래, 다니면서 멋진 자연 풍경을 많이 봤어.
M: 흥미로운 장소에도 많이 들렀니?
W: 물론이지. 가는 길에 멋진 마을들이 있었어.

(a) 최근 휴가에서 여자가 한 일
(b) 여자가 장거리 자동차 여행을 하기로 결정하게 된 과정
(c) 여자가 장거리 자동차 여행 중에 즐긴 것
(d) 여자가 다가오는 휴가를 보낼 방법

정답 (a)

해설 　대화의 주제를 묻는 문제이다. 남자가 휴가를 보내고 돌아온 여자에게 휴가가 어땠는지(How was your vacation?) 묻자, 2주 동안 차를 몰고 전국을 다니면서 멋진 자연 풍경을 많이 보고(I saw some great natural scenery along the way.) 몇몇 멋진 마을에 들렀다(There were some great towns along the route.)고 했다. 따라서 (a)가 정답이다.

어휘 　mainly adv. 주로 discuss v. 논의하다 back adv. 돌아와서 vacation n. 휴가 amazing adj. 굉장한 spend v. 보내다 drive v. 차를 몰다 cross-country adv. 전국으로 횡단하여 really adv. 정말로 cover a lot of ground phr. 여기저기 돌아다니다 great adj. 멋진 natural adj. 자연의 scenery n. 풍경 stop v. 들르다 interesting adj. 흥미로운 place n. 장소 of course idm. 물론 town n. 마을 route n. 경로 recent adj. 최근의 decide to do col. ~하기로 결정하다 take a road trip col. 장거리 자동차 여행을 하다 upcoming adj. 다가오는

06 　대화의 내용과 일치하는 것 | 불만 사항 　　　　　　　　　　난이도 ★☆☆

Listen to a conversation. What is the woman's complaint about her current hotel room? W: Hi, I'm staying in room 702. I'm wondering if I can switch rooms. M: Is there anything wrong with your current room, ma'am? W: It smells like sweaty socks—I really can't stand it. M: Oh, is it coming from the air-conditioner, or the drain, maybe? W: I'm not sure. You'll have to check for yourself. M: OK, I'll send someone up—and in the meantime, I'll arrange a new room for you. **(a) It has an unpleasant smell.** (b) The air conditioner is broken. (c) The drain is not working properly. (d) She found a pair of dirty socks in it.	대화를 들어 보시오. 여자가 현재의 호텔 방에 관해 불평하고 있는 것은? W: 안녕하세요, 저는 702호에 묵고 있습니다. 방을 바꿀 수 있을지 모르겠네요. M: 현재 묵고 계신 방에 어떤 문제가 있나요, 손님? W: 땀에 젖은 양말 같은 냄새가 나서요-정말 못 참겠어요. M: 아, 혹시 냄새가 에어컨에서 나나요, 아니면 배수구에서 나나요? W: 잘 모르겠어요. 직접 확인해 보셔야 할 것 같아요. M: 알겠습니다, 사람을 보내 드릴게요-그사이에 새 방을 준비해 드리겠습니다. **(a) 불쾌한 냄새가 난다.** (b) 에어컨이 고장났다. (c) 배수구가 제대로 작동하지 않는다. (d) 여자가 더러운 양말 한 켤레를 발견했다.

정답 　(a)

해설 　여자가 하는 불평이 무엇인지를 묻는 문제이다. 여자가 방을 바꿀 수 있는지 묻자, 남자가 현재 방에 문제가 있는지 물었다. 여자는 방에서 땀에 젖은 양말 같은 냄새가 나서 참을 수 없다(It smells like sweaty socks-I really can't stand it.)고 했다. 따라서 It smells like sweaty socks를 바꿔 표현한 (a)가 정답이다.

<mark>**Paraphrasing**</mark> 　It smells like sweaty socks. → It has an unpleasant smell.

어휘 　complaint n. 불평 current adj. 현재의 stay v. 묵다 wonder v. 궁금하다 switch v. 바꾸다 wrong adj. 잘못된 smell v. 냄새가 나다 sweaty adj. 땀에 젖은 socks n. 양말 stand v. 참다 air-conditioner n. 에어컨 drain n. 배수구 check v. 확인하다 send v. 보내다 in the meantime phr. 그사이에 arrange v. 준비하다 unpleasant adj. 불쾌한 broken adj. 고장난 properly adv. 제대로 find v. 발견하다 dirty adj. 더러운 pair n. 한 켤레

Listen to a conversation. Which is correct about the woman?

M: Good morning, Carrie. Did you do anything fun last night?
W: Hi, Peter. I had a couple of friends come over to watch the movie *Casablanca*.
M: Oh, I love old classics. Had you seen that one before?
W: Yeah, it's my favorite movie. My friends hadn't, though—they're not really into classics.
M: Really? Were you able to change their minds about them?
W: No. They both said that they couldn't understand why I love them—they think classic movies are boring.

(a) She went to a friend's house to watch *Casablanca*.
(b) She watched *Casablanca* for the first time last night.
(c) She and the man are both fans of classic films.
(d) She changed her friends' opinion of old movies.

대화를 들어 보시오. 여자에 관해 대화의 내용과 일치하는 것은?

M: 안녕, 캐리. 어젯밤에 재미있게 보냈어?
W: 안녕, 피터. 친구 두 명을 불러서 <카사블랑카>라는 영화를 봤어.
M: 아, 나는 오래된 고전을 좋아해. 전에 그 영화를 본 적이 있어?
W: 그래, 내가 제일 좋아하는 영화야. 하지만 내 친구들은 그렇지 않았어-그들은 정말로 고전에 관심이 없어.
M: 정말? 고전에 관한 그들의 생각을 바꿀 수 있었니?
W: 아니. 둘 다 내가 고전을 사랑하는 이유를 이해할 수 없다고 했어-그들은 고전 영화가 지루하다고 생각해.

(a) 여자는 친구 집에 가서 <카사블랑카>를 봤다.
(b) 여자는 어젯밤에 처음으로 <카사블랑카>를 봤다.
(c) 여자와 남자는 둘 다 고전 영화의 팬이다.
(d) 여자는 오래된 영화에 관한 친구들의 생각을 바꿨다.

정답 (c)

해설 여자에 관해 대화문의 내용과 일치하는 것을 고르는 문제이다. 남자가 두 번째 대화문에서 오래된 고전을 좋아한다(I love old classics.)면서 여자에게 영화 *Casablanca*를 본 적이 있는지(Had you seen that one before?) 물었고 여자가 제일 좋아하는 영화라고(it's my favorite movie.) 했으므로, 둘 다 고전 영화의 팬이라는 것을 알 수 있다. 따라서 (c)가 정답이다.

어휘 correct adj. 맞는 fun adj. 재미있는 a couple of idm. 두 개(명)의 come over phr. 오다 watch v. 보다 old adj. 오래된 classic n. 고전 favorite adj. 가장 좋아하는 though conj. 하지만 really adv. 정말로 be into idm. ~에 흥미가 있다 mind n. 생각 change v. 바꾸다 both det. 둘 다 understand v. 이해하다 boring adj. 지루한 fan n. 팬 film n. 영화 opinion n. 생각

Listen to a conversation. What is wrong with the woman's meal?

W: Pardon me. I'd like to send this steak back.
M: I'm sorry. What seems to be the problem?
W: I asked specifically for it to be medium-rare—this one's well-done.
M: I'll have the chef take care of that immediately.
W: Thank you. Could I also have another glass of wine, please?
M: Of course. That will be on the house.

대화를 들어 보시오. 여자의 식사에 어떤 문제가 있는가?

W: 실례합니다. 이 스테이크를 돌려보내고 싶어요.
M: 죄송합니다. 무슨 문제가 있나요?
W: 저는 특별히 약간 익혀 달라고 요청했는데-이건 완전히 익었어요.
M: 요리사가 바로 처리하도록 하겠습니다.
W: 고맙습니다. 와인도 한 잔 더 주시겠어요?
M: 물론입니다. 그건 무료로 제공해 드리겠습니다.

(a) Her steak was overcooked.
(b) Her steak was smaller than expected.
(c) She received the wrong side dish with her steak.
(d) She did not receive a glass of wine with her steak.

(a) 여자의 스테이크가 너무 많이 익었다.
(b) 여자의 스테이크가 예상보다 작다.
(c) 여자는 스테이크와 함께 잘못된 곁들임 요리를 받았다.
(d) 여자는 스테이크와 함께 와인을 받지 못했다.

정답 (a)

해설 여자의 식사에 어떤 문제가 있는지 묻는 문제이다. 두 번째 대화문에서, 여자는 스테이크를 약간 익혀 달라고 요청했지만 완전히 익은 스테이크를 제공받았다고 했다(I asked specifically for it to be medium-rare-this one's well-done.). 따라서 be well-done을 be overcooked로 바꿔 표현한 (a)가 정답이다.

Paraphrasing be well-done → be overcooked

어휘 wrong adj. 잘못된 meal n. 식사 pardon me idm. 죄송합니다 send back phr. 돌려보내다 problem n. 문제 ask v. 요청하다 specifically adv. 특별히 medium-rare adj. 약간 익힌 well-done adj. 완전히 익힌 chef n. 요리사 take care of phr. ~을 처리하다 immediately adv. 즉시 glass n. 한 잔(의 양) wine n. 와인 of course idm. 물론 on the house idm. 무료로 제공되는 overcook v. 너무 오래 익히다 expect v. 예상하다 receive v. 받다 side dish n. 곁들임 요리

09 말의 목적, 주제, 요지 | 요지

난이도 ★☆☆

Listen to an announcement. What is mainly being advertised about the workshop?

Unlock your imagination with a two-day fantasy writer's workshop at Blackwell College! Have you ever dreamed of learning directly from published fantasy authors? Now's your chance! This workshop will be led by Tom Barker and Susan Marshall, two of the country's leading writers of fantasy fiction. Discover their advanced techniques of world-building, character development, and plot structure—all while receiving personalized instruction. Visit our website to register!

(a) It will explore the works of two leading fantasy writers.
(b) It will guide participants through the publishing process.
(c) It will provide an overview of recent trends in the fantasy genre.
(d) It will enable attendees to learn directly from published authors.

공지를 들어 보시오. 워크숍에 관해 주로 광고하고 있는 것은?

블랙웰 대학에서 이틀간 열리는 판타지 작가 워크숍에서 상상의 나래를 펼쳐 보세요! 기성 판타지 작가들에게서 직접 배우는 것을 꿈꿔 본 적이 있나요? 이제 그 기회가 왔습니다! 이 워크숍은 국내 판타지 소설 분야의 두 중견 작가인 톰 바커와 수전 마셜이 주재합니다. 그들이 세계관을 구축하고 캐릭터를 개발하고 플롯을 짜는 고급 기법 모두를 개인별 맞춤 지도를 받으면서 발견하세요. 우리 웹사이트를 방문해서 등록하세요!

(a) 중견 판타지 작가 두 명의 작품을 탐구할 것이다.
(b) 참가자들에게 출판 과정을 설명해 줄 것이다.
(c) 판타지 장르의 최근 추세에 관한 개요를 제공할 것이다.
(d) 참가자들이 기성 작가들에게서 직접 배울 수 있을 것이다.

정답 (d)

해설 광고의 주제를 묻는 문제이다. Blackwell College에서 열리는 판타지 작가 워크숍을 중견 작가인 Tom Barker와 Susan Marshall이 주재하며, 이 둘이 직접 참석자에게 개인별 맞춤 지도를 할 것(Discover their advanced techniques of world-building, character development, and plot structure-all while receiving personalized instruction.)이라는 내용의 광고이다. 따라서 (d)가 정답이다.

어휘 announcement n. 공지 mainly adv. 주로 advertise v. 광고하다 workshop n. 워크숍 unlock v. 열다 imagination n. 상상력 fantasy adj. 판타지의 writer n. 작가 college n. 대학 dream of phr. ~을 꿈꾸다 learn v. 배우다 directly adv. 직접 published adj. 출판된 author n. 작가 chance n. 기회 lead v. 이끌다 country n. 나라 leading adj. 중견의 fiction n. 소설 discover v. 발견하다 advanced adj. 고급의 technique n. 기법 world-building n. 세계 구축 character n. 캐릭터 development n. 개발 plot n. 플롯 structure n. 구조 personalized instruction col. 개인별 맞춤 지도 visit v. 방문하다 website n. 웹사이트 register v. 등록하다 explore v. 탐구하다 work n. 작품 guide v. 설명하다 participant n. 참가자 publishing n. 출판 process n. 과정 provide v. 제공하다 overview n. 개요 recent adj. 최근의 trend n. 추세 genre n. 장르 enable A to do col. A가 ~할 수 있게 하다 attendee n. 참석자

10 말의 목적, 주제, 요지 | 주제

난이도 ★★★

Listen to a lecture. What is the main topic of the lecture?

Welcome, everyone. In today's lecture, I'll discuss the wide variety of life in desert ecosystems. Many plant and animal species have evolved to cope with challenging desert conditions by tapping into precious water supplies and avoiding burning sunlight. For instance, desert plants often possess far-reaching roots that give them access to deeply buried water sources. Many desert animals have learned to burrow underground to get away from intense daytime sunlight and to limit their hydration needs.

(a) The adaption of desert species to their harsh environment
(b) The interaction of different species in desert ecosystems
(c) The reason for the small number of desert species
(d) The effect of climate change on desert species

강의를 들어 보시오. 강의의 주제는 무엇인가?

여러분, 환영합니다. 오늘 강의에서는 사막 생태계의 매우 다양한 생물에 관해 이야기하겠습니다. 여러 식물과 동물 종은 소중한 물 공급을 활용하고 뜨거운 햇빛을 피함으로써 가혹한 사막 환경에 대처하도록 진화했습니다. 예를 들어, 사막 식물은 보통 깊숙이 묻힌 수원에 접근할 수 있도록 멀리까지 뻗은 뿌리를 가지고 있습니다. 많은 사막 동물은 강렬한 낮의 햇빛에서 벗어나고 수분 요구를 줄이기 위해 땅속으로 파고 들어가서 사는 법을 배웠습니다.

(a) 가혹한 환경에 적응하는 사막의 종들
(b) 사막 생태계에서 다른 종들의 상호 작용
(c) 사막 종들의 수가 적은 이유
(d) 기후 변화가 사막 종들에 미치는 영향

정답 (a)

해설 강의의 주제를 묻는 문제이다. 강의 초반에 사막 생태계의 매우 다양한 생물을 주제로 이야기하겠다(I'll discuss the wide variety of life in desert ecosystems.)고 한 뒤에 여러 사막 식물과 동물 종이 가혹한 사막 환경에 적응하는 방법을 예를 들어 설명했다. 따라서 (a)가 정답이다.

어휘 lecture n. 강의 main adj. 주요한 topic n. 주제 a wide variety of col. 매우 다양한 life n. 생물 desert n. 사막 ecosystem n. 생태계 plant n. 식물 animal n. 동물 species n. 종 evolve v. 진화하다 cope with phr. ~에 대처하다 challenging adj. 힘든 conditions pl. 환경 tap into phr. ~을 활용하다 precious adj. 소중한 water supply n. 물 공급 avoid v. 피하다 burning adj. 뜨거운 sunlight n. 햇빛 for instance idm. 예를 들어 possess v. 가지고 있다 far-reaching adj. 멀리까지 미치는 root n. 뿌리 give A access to B col. A가 B에 접근할 수 있게 하다 deeply adv. 깊이 buried adj. 파묻힌 water source col. 수원 learn v. 배우다 burrow v. 파다 underground adv. 땅 속으로 get away from phr. ~로부터 벗어나다 intense adj. 강렬한 daytime n. 낮 limit v. 제한하다 hydration n. 수분 needs pl. 요구 adaption n. 적응 harsh adj. 혹독한 environment n. 환경 interaction n. 상호 작용 different adj. 다른 effect n. 영향 climate n. 기후 change n. 변화

11 말의 내용과 일치하는 것 | 일치

Listen to a weather forecast. Which is correct according to the forecast?

Now for your local weather forecast. Bring your umbrella tomorrow, as heavy rains and high winds are expected to start around 8 a.m. in Oakville. These will die down in the afternoon, giving way to clear skies by around 7 p.m. Temperatures tomorrow will reach a high of 23 degrees Celsius in the afternoon, but expect them to fall sharply after the rains pass—so you might need a sweater if you go out after dark.

(a) The rain is forecast to start tomorrow afternoon.
(b) The clouds will have largely disappeared by the evening.
(c) The temperature will fall to as low as 23 degrees tomorrow.
(d) The end of the rain will gradually bring higher temperatures.

일기 예보를 들어 보시오. 일기 예보의 내용과 일치하는 것은?

우리 지역 일기 예보 시간입니다. 내일은 오전 8시경에 큰비와 강한 바람이 오크빌에서 시작될 것으로 예상되오니 우산을 가져가시기 바랍니다. 큰비와 강한 바람은 오후에 점차 잦아들어 오후 7시경에는 맑은 하늘이 될 것입니다. 내일의 기온은 오후에 섭씨 23도까지 오르겠지만, 비가 그치고 나면 기온이 급격히 떨어질 것으로 예상되므로, 해가 진 뒤에 외출하신다면 스웨터가 필요할 수도 있습니다.

(a) 내일 오후에 비가 내리기 시작할 것으로 예상된다.
(b) 구름은 저녁에 대부분 걷힐 것이다.
(c) 내일의 기온은 최저 섭씨 23도까지 떨어질 것이다.
(d) 비가 그치면 서서히 기온이 오를 것이다.

정답 (b)

해설 일기 예보의 내용과 일치하는 것을 묻는 문제이다. 일기 예보 중반에 큰비와 강한 바람이 오후에 점차 잦아들어 오후 7시경에는 맑은 하늘이 될 것(These will die down in the afternoon, giving way to clear skies by around 7 p.m.)이라고 했다. 따라서 Heavy rains and high winds will give way to clear skies by around 7 p.m.을 바꿔 표현한 (b)가 정답이다.

Paraphrasing Heavy rains and high winds will give way to clear skies by around 7 p.m.
→ The clouds will have largely disappeared by the evening.

어휘 weather n. 일기 forecast n. 예보; v. 예측하다 now for idm. 자 이제 ~으로 넘어가겠다 local adj. 지역의 bring v. 가져가다 umbrella n. 우산 heavy rain col. 큰비 high wind col. 강한 바람 be expected to do col. ~할 것으로 예상되다 start v. 시작되다 around prep. ~경 die down phr. 차츰 잦아들다 give way to phr. ~로 바뀌다 clear adj. 맑은 sky n. 하늘 temperature n. 기온 reach v. ~에 이르다 degree n. 도(온도의 단위) Celsius n. 섭씨 but conj. 하지만 fall v. 떨어지다 sharply adv. 급격히 pass v. 지나가다 so conj. 그래서 might aux. ~할지도 모른다 need v. 필요하다 sweater n. 스웨터 if conj. 만약 ~라면 go out phr. 외출하다 after dark col. 해가 진 뒤에 cloud n. 구름 largely adv. 대부분 disappear v. 사라지다 gradually adv. 서서히

12 말의 내용과 일치하는 것 | 일치

Listen to a talk. Which is correct according to the talk?

Thank you for attending today's talk. When answering questions that require significant mental processing, people instinctively look away from the face of their questioner. Studies show that this behavior is actually beneficial—adults instructed to maintain eye contact perform less effectively on intellectual tasks than those allowed to avert their gaze. Children are less likely to look

강연을 들어 보시오. 강연의 내용과 일치하는 것은?

오늘의 강연에 참석해 주셔서 감사합니다. 중요한 정신적 처리를 필요로 하는 질문에 대답할 때, 사람들은 높은 질문자의 얼굴을 본능적으로 피합니다. 연구 결과, 이러한 행동은 실제로 유익하다고 나타났습니다. 눈맞춤 유지하도록 지시 받은 성인들은 지시 받지 않은 사람들보다 지적 과제에서 덜 효과적인 성과를 보입니다. 어린

away spontaneously, but they also perform better when trained to avoid eye contact. These findings suggest that human faces trigger heavy mental processing and that this processing negatively affects the ability to think through other tasks.

(a) Adults prefer consistent eye contact during intellectual discussions.
(b) Children are less likely than adults to maintain eye contact.
(c) Avoiding eye contact does not help children on tasks.
(d) Processing human faces is a mentally challenging task.

이들은 스스로 눈을 피하는 경향이 적지만, 눈빛을 피하는 훈련을 받을 경우 더 나은 성과를 내는 것으로 나타났습니다. 이러한 연구 결과는 인간의 얼굴이 상당한 수준의 정신적 처리를 유발하며, 이러한 처리가 다른 과제를 생각하는 능력에 부정적인 영향을 미친다는 것을 시사합니다.

(a) 성인들은 지적인 토론 중에 일관성 있게 시선을 마주치기를 선호한다.
(b) 아이들은 계속 시선을 유지할 가능성이 성인들보다 더 작다.
(c) 시선을 피하는 것은 아이들의 작업에 도움이 되지 않는다.
(d) 인간의 얼굴을 사고 처리하는 것은 정신적으로 힘든 작업이다.

정답 (d)

해설 강연의 내용과 일치하는 것을 묻는 문제이다. 강연 초반에 상당한 사고 처리 과정을 요구하는 질문에 답할 때 사람들이 본능적으로 질문자의 얼굴로부터 눈길을 돌린다(When answering questions that require significant mental processing, people instinctively look away from the face of their questioner.)고 했고, 다음 문장에서 눈을 마주치는 것보다 눈을 피하는 것이 지적인 작업에 유익하다(Studies show that this behavior is actually beneficial—adults instructed to maintain eye contact perform less effectively on intellectual tasks than those allowed to avert their gaze.)는 연구 결과를 제시했다. 따라서 시선 처리가 정신적으로 힘든 작업이라는 것을 알 수 있으므로 (d)가 정답이다.

Paraphrasing These findings suggest that human faces trigger heavy mental processing and that this processing negatively affects the ability to think through other tasks.
→ Processing human faces is a mentally challenging task.

어휘 talk n. 강연 attend v. 참석하다 answer v. 답하다 question n. 질문 require v. 요구하다 significant adj. 상당한 mental processing 사고 처리 과정 instinctively adv. 본능적으로 look away from phr. ~로부터 눈길을 돌리다 face n. 얼굴 questioner n. 질문자 study n. 연구 show v. 보여 주다 behavior n. 행동 actually adv. 실제로는 beneficial adj. 유익한 adult n. 성인 instruct v. 지시하다 maintain v. 유지하다 eye contact col. 시선을 마주침 perform v. 수행하다, 성과를 내다 effectively adv. 효과적으로 intellectual adj. 지적인 task n. 작업 allow v. 허락하다 avert v. 피하다 gaze n. 시선 likely adv. ~할 것 같은 spontaneously adv. 자발적으로 train v. 훈련하다 avoid v. 피하다 findings n. 결과 suggest v. 시사하다 human adj. 인간의 trigger v. 유발하다 heavy adj. 심한 negatively adv. 부정적으로 affect v. 영향을 미치다 ability n. 능력 think through phr. ~을 충분히 생각하다, 신중히 고려하다 other adj. 다른 prefer v. 선호하다 consistent eye contact col. 시선을 유지하는 discussion n. 토론 process v. 처리하다 mentally adv. 정신적으로 challenging adj. 힘든

13 글의 목적, 주제, 요지 | 목적

난이도 ★☆☆

What is the main purpose of John's email?

Dear Lauren,

When you agreed to keep an eye on my house during my vacation, I had no idea that you'd do a bunch of chores in my absence. I noticed that you collected my mail and tended to my garden. I can't tell you how much I appreciate all your help! In particular, I'm very grateful to you for removing the leaves that were clogging my drains. I can't imagine what would've happened had they been clogged up during that big rainstorm. Please let me know if I can return the favor sometime!

John

(a) To give Lauren a list of things to do during his trip
(b) To offer Lauren advice about preparing for a storm
(c) To inform Lauren of maintenance issues with his house
(d) To thank Lauren for looking after his home during his trip

존이 보낸 이메일의 주요 목적은 무엇인가?

로런에게,

당신이 제 휴가 기간에 우리 집을 계속 지켜봐 주겠다고 동의하셨을 때, 제가 없는 동안 여러 가지 일을 해 주실 줄은 몰랐습니다. 제 우편물을 수거하고 정원을 돌봐 주셨다는 것을 알게 되었습니다. 당신의 모든 도움에 얼마나 감사한지 말로 다할 수 없습니다! 특히, 우리 집 배수구를 막고 있던 나뭇잎을 치워 주셔서 정말 고맙습니다. 그 큰 폭풍우 동안 배수구가 막혔더라면 어떤 일이 벌어졌을지 상상조차 할 수 없습니다. 언제쯤 은혜를 갚을 수 있을지 알려 주시면 좋겠습니다!

존

(a) 로런에게 자기가 여행하는 동안 할 일 목록을 주려고
(b) 로런에게 폭풍우에 대비하는 방법을 조언하려고
(c) 로런에게 자기 집의 유지 보수 문제를 알리려고
(d) 로런에게 자기가 여행하는 동안 집을 돌봐 준 것에 대한 고마움을 전하려고

정답 (d)

해설 이메일을 보낸 주된 목적을 묻는 문제이다. 이메일 중반에서 John이 휴가 간 동안 Lauren이 해 준 일에 크게 고마워하고 있다(I can't tell you how much I appreciate all your help!)는 것을 알 수 있으며, 앞뒤로 Lauren이 John의 집 우편물을 수거하고 정원을 돌봐 준 것과 배수구를 막고 있던 나뭇잎을 치워 준 것을 도움의 예로 들었다. 이를 통해 이메일을 보낸 주된 목적은 John이 휴가를 떠난 동안 집을 돌봐 준 것에 대해 Lauren에게 고마움을 전하려는 것임을 알 수 있다. 따라서 (d)가 정답이다.

Paraphrasing I can't tell you how much I appreciate all your help!
→ To thank Lauren for looking after his home during his trip

어휘 keep an eye on idm. ~을 계속 지켜보다 vacation n. 휴가 have no idea that ~ idm. ~을 전혀 몰랐다 a bunch of idm. 여러 가지 chore n. 일 in one's absence idm. ~이 없는 동안 notice v. 알아차리다 collect v. 수거하다 mail n. 우편물 tend to phr. ~을 돌보다 garden n. 정원 appreciate v. 고마워하다 help n. 도움 in particular phr. 특히 grateful adj. 고마워하는 remove v. 치우다 leaf n. 나뭇잎(pl. leaves) clog (up) v. 막다 drain n. 배수구 imagine v. 상상하다 happen v. 일어나다 rainstorm n. 폭풍우 return the favor idm. 은혜를 갚다 sometime adv. 언젠가 list n. 목록 trip n. 여행 offer v. 제공하다 advice n. 조언 prepare for phr. ~을 준비하다 storm n. 폭풍우 inform v. 알리다 maintenance n. 유지 보수 issue n. 문제 look after phr. 돌보다

What is mainly being advertised?

Get ready for the ultimate thrill! Introducing the Star Racer, the all-new roller coaster at Thriller Theme Park! Feel the rush of a lifetime as you fly at rocket speed through gravity-defying twists, turns, and loops on this one-of-a-kind spaceship-themed ride. Join us for the grand opening on October 1 and be among the first to reach the stars. Get your Thriller Theme Park tickets today at thrillerthemepark.com!

(a) The opening of a theme park's new ride
(b) A discount on tickets to a new theme park
(c) The start of the new season at a theme park
(d) An event to celebrate a theme park's opening

주로 광고하고 있는 것은?

최고의 스릴에 대비하세요! 스릴러 테마파크의 완전히 새로운 롤러코스터, 스타 레이서를 소개합니다! 이 특별한 우주선 테마의 놀이기구에서 중력을 거스르는 꼬임, 회전, 고리 궤도를 로켓 속도로 날아가면서 평생 잊지 못할 흥분을 느껴 보세요. 10월 1일 개장식에 참여해서 최초로 별에 도달하는 사람 중 한 명이 되어 보세요. 오늘 thrillerthemepark.com에서 스릴러 테마파크 입장권을 구매하세요!

(a) 테마파크의 새로운 놀이기구 공개
(b) 새로운 테마파크 입장권 할인
(c) 테마파크의 새로운 시즌 시작
(d) 테마파크 개장을 축하하는 행사

정답 (a)

해설 광고의 주제를 묻는 문제이다. Thriller Theme Park에서 새롭게 선보이는 롤러코스터인 Star Racer를 소개하고 있으며 (Introducing the Star Racer, the all-new roller coaster at Thriller Theme Park!), 10월 1일에 개장식을 할 예정이라고 했다(Join us for the grand opening on October 1 and be among the first to reach the stars.). 따라서 (a)가 정답이다.

Paraphrasing Introducing the Star Racer, the all-new roller coaster at Thriller Theme Park! Join us for the grand opening on October 1 and be among the first to reach the stars.
→ The opening of a theme park's new ride

어휘 get ready for phr. ~에 대비하다 ultimate adj. 최고의 thrill n. 스릴 introduce v. 소개하다 roller coaster n. 롤러코스터 theme park n. 테마파크 rush n. 흥분 lifetime n. 일생 fly v. 날다 rocket n. 로켓 speed n. 속도 gravity-defying adj. 중력을 거스르는 twist n. 꼬임 turn n. 회전 loop n. 고리 one-of-a-kind adj. 특별한 spaceship-themed adj. 우주선 테마의 ride n. 놀이기구 join v. 참여하다 grand opening col. 개장식 among prep. ~중에 reach v. 도달하다 get v. 구매하다 ticket n. 입장권 today adv. 오늘 discount n. 할인 start n. 시작 season n. 시즌 event n. 행사 celebrate v. 축하하다

What is the main purpose of the passage?

The dangers on the Internet are a source of much concern for parents. However, parents can safeguard their children by taking a few precautions. To start, parents should place the family computer in an area of the home that is easily monitored. They should also set limits on the amount of time that their children are allowed to spend on the computer. Most importantly, parents must keep the lines of communication open with their children and encourage their children to express concerns freely.

지문의 주요 목적은 무엇인가?

인터넷의 위험은 부모들에게 많은 걱정의 원천입니다. 하지만 부모들은 몇 가지 예방 조치를 취해 자녀를 보호할 수 있습니다. 먼저, 부모들은 가족 컴퓨터를 집 안에서 쉽게 모니터링할 수 있는 곳에 두어야 합니다. 또한 자녀가 컴퓨터를 사용할 수 있는 시간을 제한해야 합니다. 무엇보다도 부모들은 자녀와의 의사소통 수단을 계속 열어 두고서 자녀가 자유롭게 고민을 표현하도록 권장해야 합니다.

(a) To explain the negative effect of online activity on children
(b) To suggest ways of protecting children from online dangers
(c) To advise parents to talk to their children about Internet safety
(d) To warn parents about the risks of unsupervised Internet use for children

(a) 온라인 활동이 아이들에게 미치는 부정적인 영향을 설명하려고
(b) 온라인의 위험에서 아이들을 보호하는 방법을 제안하려고
(c) 부모들에게 인터넷 안전에 관해 자녀와 이야기하도록 조언하려고
(d) 부모들에게 감독 없는 인터넷 사용의 위험성을 경고하려고

정답 (b)

해설 지문의 주요 목적을 묻는 문제이다. 지문 초반에 부모들이 몇 가지 예방 조치를 취함으로써 자녀를 보호할 수 있다 (However, parents can safeguard their children by taking a few precautions.)고 한 다음, 예방 조치를 차례로 제시하고 있다. 따라서 (b)가 정답이다.

Paraphrasing However, parents can safeguard their children by taking a few precautions.
→ To suggest ways of protecting children from online dangers

어휘 danger n. 위험 source n. 원인 concern n. 걱정, 고민 parent n. 부모 however adv. 하지만 safeguard v. 보호하다 take v. 취하다 precaution n. 예방 조치 start v. 시작하다 place v. 두다 area n. 구역 easily adv. 쉽게 monitor v. 감시하다 set v. 설정하다 limit n. 제한 amount n. 양 be allowed to do col. ~하는 것이 허용되다 spend v. 시간을 보내다 most importantly idm. 가장 중요한 것은 keep v. 유지하다 line n. 선 communication n. 의사소통 open adj. 열린 encourage A to do col. A에게 ~하라고 권하다 express v. 표현하다 freely adv. 자유롭게 explain v. 설명하다 negative adj. 부정적인 effect n. 영향 activity n. 활동 suggest v. 제안하다 way n. 방법 protect v. 보호하다 advise v. 조언하다 talk v. 이야기하다 safety n. 안전 warn v. 경고하다 risk n. 위험 unsupervised adj. 감독 없는 use n. 사용

16 | 글의 목적, 주제, 요지 | 주제

난이도 ★★☆

What is the main topic of the passage?

In the 1850s, American settlers in the Pacific Northwest befriended a Native American man named Si'ahl, who was a leader of the local Duwamish and Suquamish tribes. Si'ahl and his followers traded with the settlers and helped them survive the difficult conditions on the frontier. To prevent conflict, Si'ahl negotiated peaceful relations with the inhabitants of the new community, which at the time was known as Duwamps. In honor of Si'ahl, the settlers eventually renamed their settlement "Seattle," which soon became an important hub for commercial activity in the region.

(a) The origins of trade among Native Americans in the Pacific Northwest
(b) The adaptation of settlers to life among the tribes of the Pacific Northwest
(c) A town's role in resolving a conflict between Native Americans and settlers
(d) A Native American leader's role in the development of a frontier settlement

지문의 주제는 무엇인가?

1850년대, 태평양 북서부에 정착한 미국인들은 현지 두와미시와 수쿼미시 부족의 지도자인 시아흘이라는 북미 원주민 남자와 친구가 되었다. 시아흘과 그의 추종자들은 정착민들과 무역하며 정착민들이 개척 지역의 힘든 환경에서 살아남을 수 있도록 도왔다. 충돌을 방지하기 위해 시아흘은 당시 듀웜프스라고 알려져 있던 새로운 지역 사회의 주민들과 평화적인 관계를 협상했다. 시아흘을 기리기 위해 정착민들은 결국 정착지 이름을 "시애틀"로 바꾸었고, 이곳은 곧 이 지역에서 상업 활동의 중요한 중심지가 되었다.

(a) 태평양 북서부 북미 원주민들 간 무역의 기원
(b) 태평양 북서부 부족들 사이에서 사는 것에 대한 정착민들의 생활 적응
(c) 북미 원주민들과 정착민들 간의 충돌을 해결하는 도시의 역할
(d) 개척 지역 정착지 발전에서 북미 원주민 지도자의 역할

정답 (d)

해설 지문의 주제를 묻는 문제이다. 지문 초반에 Si'ahl이라는 북미 원주민 부족 지도자와 추종자들이 정착민들과 무역하며 그 정착민들이 개척 지역의 힘든 환경에서 살아남을 수 있도록 도왔다(Si'ahl and his followers traded with the settlers and helped them survive the difficult conditions on the frontier.)고 한 다음, 후반에 Si'ahl을 기리기 위해 이름을 바꾼 Seattle이 상업 활동의 중심지가 되었다(In honor of Si'ahl, the settlers eventually renamed their settlement "Seattle," which soon became an important hub for commercial activity in the region.)고 했다. 따라서 지문의 주요 내용은 북미 원주민 지도자 Si'ahl이 개척 지역 정착지의 발전에 어떻게 기여했는지에 관한 것이므로 (d)가 정답이다.

어휘 settler n. 정착민 Pacific Northwest n. 태평양 북서부 befriend v. 친구가 되다 Native American n. 북미 원주민 leader n. 지도자 local adj. 현지의 tribe n. 부족 follower n. 추종자 trade v. 무역하다; n. 무역 survive v. 살아남다 difficult adj. 힘든 condition n. 환경 frontier n. 개척 지역 prevent v. 방지하다 conflict n. 충돌 negotiate v. 협상하다 peaceful adj. 평화적인 relation n. 관계 inhabitant n. 주민 community n. 지역 사회 at the time adv. 당시에 be known as phr. ~로 알려져 있다 in honor of col. ~을 기리기 위해 eventually adv. 결국에는 rename v. 이름을 바꾸다 settlement n. 정착지 become v. 되다 important adj. 중요한 hub n. 중심지 commercial adj. 상업의 activity n. 활동 region n. 지역 origin n. 기원 among prep. ~사이에 adaptation n. 적응 life n. 삶 town n. 도시 role n. 역할 resolve v. 해결하다 development n. 발전

17 글의 내용과 일치하는 것 | 일치   난이도 ★★☆

Which of the following is correct about Fantasy Eggs?

The Enchanta Toy Corporation, famous for children's toys and games such as Nanomal Electronic Pets and Tiger-Bear trading cards, has introduced a new item that is proving even more popular among adults than among children. Fantasy Eggs are small chocolate eggs, each containing a small plastic figure shaped like a fantastic creature. Originally created as treats for youngsters, the eggs are now widely sought after by adult collectors, who have been scrambling to find all 131 figures. It has been estimated that over 5 million Fantasy Eggs are purchased each month, with young women between 18 and 20 being the most enthusiastic collectors.

(a) They were originally marketed to adults.
(b) They contain animal-shaped chocolate figures.
(c) They are mostly purchased as collectibles.
(d) They are more popular among men than women.

다음 중 판타지 에그에 관해 지문의 내용과 일치하는 것은?

나노멀 일렉트로닉 펫과 타이거-베어 트레이딩 카드 같은 어린이용 장난감과 게임으로 유명한 엔찬타 토이 사는 아이들보다 어른들 사이에서 훨씬 더 인기 있는 것으로 드러나고 있는 신제품을 소개했습니다. 판타지 에그는 작은 초콜릿 달걀로, 각 달걀에는 환상적인 생물 모양의 작은 플라스틱 피규어가 들어 있습니다. 원래 어린이들을 위한 간식으로 만들어졌지만, 이제 성인 수집가들이 널리 찾고 있으며, 그들은 131개의 피규어를 모두 찾기 위해 바쁘게 움직이고 있습니다. 매달 500만 개 이상의 판타지 에그가 판매되고 있으며, 18세에서 20세 사이의 젊은 여성들이 가장 열정적인 수집가들로 추정되고 있습니다.

(a) 원래 어른들을 대상으로 판매되었다.
(b) 동물 모양의 초콜릿 피규어가 들어 있다.
(c) 대부분 수집품으로 구매된다.
(d) 여성보다 남성에게서 더 인기가 있다.

정답 (c)

해설 판타지 에그에 관해 지문의 내용과 일치하는 것을 고르는 문제이다. 지문에서 판타지 에그는 원래 어린이들을 위한 간식으로 만들어졌지만, 이제 성인 수집가들이 널리 찾고 있으며, 그들은 131개의 피규어를 모두 찾기 위해 빠르게 움직이고 있다(Originally created as treats for youngsters, the eggs are now widely sought after by adult collectors, who have been scrambling to find all 131 figures.)고 했다. 따라서 (c)가 정답이다.

Paraphrasing the eggs are now widely sought after by adult collectors
→ They are mostly purchased as collectibles.

어휘 correct adj. 맞는 fantasy n. 공상 egg n. 달걀 toy n. 장난감 corporation n. 회사 famous adj. 유명한 game n. 게임 such as col. ~와 같은 electronic adj. 전자의 pet n. 반려동물 trading card n. 트레이딩 카드 introduce v. 소개하다 item n. 품목 prove v. 드러나다 popular adj. 인기 있는 adult n. 어른 small adj. 작은 chocolate n. 초콜릿 contain v. ~이 들어 있다 plastic n. 플라스틱 figure n. 피규어 shaped adj. ~모양의 fantastic adj. 환상적인 creature n. 생물 originally adv. 원래 create v. 만들어 내다 treat n. 간식 youngster n. 어린이 widely adv. 널리 seek after phr. ~을 찾다 adult n. 성인 collector n. 수집가 scramble v. 재빨리 움직이다 find v. 찾다 estimate v. 추산하다 purchase v. 구매하다 young adj. 젊은 between prep. ~사이 enthusiastic adj. 열정적인 market v. 판매하다 animal n. 동물 mostly adv. 대부분 collectible n. 수집품

18 | 글의 내용과 일치하는 것 | 일치

난이도 ★★★

Which of the following is correct according to the passage?

Most of Glenview University's library collection is available for general public use. Non-university members must apply for a free library card, which provides holders with access to facilities and limited borrowing privileges. Computers are publicly available at select libraries, and licensing agreements enable members of the public to access various academic resources in electronic format. The library card is not valid for access to the Warner Institute or the Rare Books Library. For specific access policies, contact individual facilities directly.

(a) Non-university members must pay a fee for a library card.
(b) All libraries have several computers set up for the public.
(c) Access to electronic resources is not available to the public.
(d) Some branches may restrict access even to library card holders.

다음 중 지문의 내용과 일치하는 것은?

글렌뷰 대학 도서관의 소장 자료 대부분은 일반 대중이 이용할 수 있습니다. 대학과 관련되지 않은 회원들은 무료 도서관 카드를 신청해야 하며, 이 카드는 소지자에게 시설 이용 권리와 제한적인 대출 권한을 제공합니다. 일부 도서관에서 컴퓨터를 공개적으로 이용할 수 있으며, 라이선스 계약을 통해 일반 회원들은 다양한 학술 자료를 전자 형식으로 이용할 수 있습니다. 도서관 카드는 워너 연구소나 희귀 도서 도서관을 이용하는 데 유효하지 않습니다. 구체적인 이용 정책을 확인하려면 각 시설에 직접 문의하십시오.

(a) 대학과 관련 없는 회원들은 도서관 카드발급 수수료를 내야 한다.
(b) 모든 도서관에는 대중을 위해 설치된 여러 대의 컴퓨터가 있다.
(c) 대중은 전자 자료를 이용할 수 없다.
(d) 일부 지점은 도서관 카드 소지자에게도 이용을 제한할 수 있다.

정답 (d)

해설 지문의 내용과 일치하는 것을 고르는 문제이다. 지문 후반에서 워너 연구소나 희귀 도서 도서관은 도서 카드로 이용할 수 없다(The library card is not valid for access to the Warner Institute or the Rare Books Library.)는 것을 알 수 있다. 따라서 이 문장을 바꿔 표현한 (d)가 정답이다.

Paraphrasing The library card is not valid for access to the Warner Institute or the Rare Books Library.
→ Some branches may restrict access even to library card holders.

어휘 correct adj. 맞는 according to prep. ~에 따르면 passage n. 지문 university n. 대학 library n. 도서관 collection n. 소장품 available adj. 이용할 수 있는 general public col. 일반 대중 use n. 이용 non-university adj. 대학과 관련되지 않은 member n. 회원 apply for phr. ~을 신청하다 free adj. 무료의 library card n. 도서 대출 카드 provide v. 제공하다 holder n. 소지자 access n. 이용 권리; v. 이용하다 facility n. 시설 limited adj. 제한된 borrowing n. 대출 privilege n. 권한 publicly adv. 공개적으로 select adj. 선택된 license v. 허가하다 agreement n. 계약 enable A to do phr. A가 ~을 할 수 있게 하다 various adj. 다양한 academic adj. 학술적인 resource n. 자료 electronic adj. 전자의 format n. 형식 valid adj. 유효한 institute n. 연구소 rare adj. 희귀한 specific adj. 구체적인 policy n. 정책 contact v. 연락하다 individual adj. 각각의 directly adv. 직접 pay v. 내다 fee n. 수수료 set up phr. 설치하다 branch n. 지점 restrict v. 제한하다 even adv. ~도

Which of the following is correct according to the announcement?

Attention Skyline Condo Residents. As part of our regular activities, Building Management will be conducting a routine maintenance check next week. An inspection team will visit apartments between 9:30 a.m. and 4 p.m. on April 12 and 13. Door locks, window locks, motion sensors, and fire detectors will be checked, and repairs will be carried out as needed at residents' expense. If you will not be home during the inspection period, the inspection team will not be able to check your property. If you would like to schedule an inspection at another time, please contact Building Management to arrange one that is suitable for you.

(a) All maintenance checks will be conducted on the same day.
(b) The cost of repairs will be covered by Building Management.
(c) The inspection team will enter homes during residents' absence.
(d) Residents may set up a maintenance check at alternative times.

다음 중 공지의 내용과 일치하는 것은?

스카이라인 아파트 주민 여러분께 알립니다. 정기적인 활동의 일환으로, 건물 관리부는 다음 주에 정기 유지 보수 점검을 시행할 예정입니다. 점검팀은 4월 12일과 13일 오전 9시 30분부터 오후 4시 사이에 아파트를 방문할 것입니다. 문 잠금장치, 창문 잠금장치, 동작 감지기, 화재 탐지기를 점검하고, 필요에 따라 주민 부담으로 수리를 시행할 것입니다. 점검 기간에 집에 없는 경우, 점검팀이 여러분의 집을 확인할 수 없을 것입니다. 다른 시간에 점검을 예약하고 싶으시다면, 건물 관리부에 연락해 여러분에게 알맞은 시간을 잡으시기 바랍니다.

(a) 모든 유지 보수 점검은 같은 날에 시행될 것이다.
(b) 수리 비용은 건물 관리부에서 부담한다.
(c) 점검팀은 거주자가 부재하는 동안 집에 들어갈 것이다.
(d) 거주자는 유지 보수 점검을 다른 시간으로 잡을 수 있다.

정답 (d)

해설 공지의 내용과 일치하는 것을 고르는 문제이다. 공지 후반에 다른 시간에 점검을 예약하고 싶다면, 건물 관리부에 연락해 본인에게 알맞은 시간을 잡기 바란다(If you would like to schedule an inspection at another time, please contact Building Management to arrange one that is suitable for you.)고 했으므로 (d)가 정답이다.

Paraphrasing schedule an inspection at another time → set up a maintenance check at alternative times

어휘 attention int. 알립니다 condo n. 아파트(= condominium) resident n. 주민 as part of col. ~의 일환으로 regular adj. 정기적인 activities pl. 활동 building n. 건물 management n. 관리진 conduct v. 시행하다 routine adj. 정기적인 maintenance n. 유지 보수 check n. 점검 inspection n. 점검 team n. 팀 visit v. 방문하다 apartment n. 아파트 between prep. ~사이에 door lock n. 문 잠금장치 window lock n. 창문 잠금장치 motion n. 동작 sensor n. 감지기 fire detector n. 화재 감지기 check v. 확인하다 repair n. 수리 carry out phr. 수행하다 as needed col. 필요에 따라 at one's expense phr. ~의 부담으로 period n. 기간 property n. 재산 would like to do col. ~하고 싶다 schedule v. 일정을 잡다 contact v. 연락하다 arrange v. 조정하다 suitable adj. 알맞은 cover v. 감당하다 enter v. 들어가다 absence n. 부재 set up phr. 마련하다 alternative adj. 대신의

According to the passage, which animal has a higher brain-size-to-body-size ratio than humans?

Brain size is not considered an indicator of the intelligence of animal species. Large-brained species—the sperm whale being the creature with the largest brain of all—tend to have very large bodies. A more reliable measure of intelligence is actually the ratio of brain size to body size. Humans have the second highest ratio of brain-size to body-size of all living creatures, followed by porpoises. Many other highly intelligent creatures—including elephants—also score highly on this metric. However, this ratio is not a perfect indicator of intelligence, either. The highest-scoring creature on this metric is the tree shrew, which comes out on top more because of its small body than because of its large brain.

(a) Sperm whales
(b) Porpoises
(c) Elephants
(d) Tree shrews

지문에 따르면, 인간보다 몸 크기 대비 뇌 크기 비율이 높은 동물은?

뇌 크기는 동물 종 지능의 지표로 간주되지 않는다. 큰 뇌를 가진 종(모든 생물 중 가장 큰 뇌를 가진 것은 향유고래이다)은 매우 큰 몸을 가지고 있다. 더 신뢰할 수 있는 지능 측정 방법은 사실 몸 크기에 대비한 뇌 크기 비율이다. 인간은 모든 살아 있는 생물 중 몸 크기 대비 뇌 크기 비율이 두 번째로 높으며, 그다음은 알락돌고래이다. 지능이 높은 다른 여러 생물들(코끼리를 포함하여)도 이 척도에서 높은 점수를 받는다. 그러나 이 비율도 지능의 완벽한 지표는 아니다. 이 척도에서 가장 높은 점수를 받은 생물은 나무두더지로, 큰 뇌 때문이기보다는 작은 몸 때문에 높은 순위를 차지하게 된다.

(a) 향유고래
(b) 알락돌고래
(c) 코끼리
(d) 나무두더지

정답   (d)

해설   인간보다 몸 크기 대비 뇌 크기 비율이 높은 동물을 묻는 문제이다. 지문 후반에서 인간보다 몸 크기 대비 뇌 크기 비율이 높은 동물이 나무두더지라는 것(The highest-scoring creature on this metric is the tree shrew.)을 알 수 있으므로 (d)가 정답이다.

Paraphrasing   second highest ratio of brain-size to body-size → second largest brain-to-body size ratio

어휘   brain n. 뇌   size n. 크기   consider v. 간주하다   indicator n. 지표   intelligence n. 지능   species n. 종   large-brained adj. 큰 뇌를 가진 sperm whale n. 향유고래   creature n. 생물   tend to do phr. ~하는 경향이 있다   body n. 몸   reliable adj. 신뢰할 수 있는   measure n. 측정 방법   actually adv. 실제로   ratio n. 비율   human n. 인간   living adj. 살아 있는   follow v. 뒤를 잇다   porpoise n. 알락돌고래   highly adv. 매우   intelligent adj. 지능이 높은   including prep. ~을 포함하여   elephant n. 코끼리   also adv. 또한   score v. 점수를 얻다   metric n. 척도   however adv. 하지만   perfect adj. 완벽한   either adv. ~도   tree shrew n. 나무두더지   come out on top idm. 이기다

Watercolor painting has acquired a reputation as an amateur pastime. However, it --------------------------. In fact, many renowned artists, from the Renaissance to modern times, have used watercolor as a major medium for their works, including John Singer Sargent, Edward Hopper, and Georgia O'Keeffe. That such prestigious artists have devoted themselves to watercolor disproves the notion that the medium is simply for hobbyists and not for serious professionals.

수채화는 아마추어의 취미로 평판을 받았다. 하지만 그것은 실제로 오랜 예술 전통의 필수적인 부분이다. 사실 르네상스부터 현대에 이르기까지 여러 유명한 화가가 수채화 물감을 작품의 주요 표현 수단으로 사용했는데 여기에는 존 싱어 사전트, 에드워드 호퍼, 조지아 오키프가 포함된다. 이렇게 명망 있는 예술가들이 수채화에 전념한 것은 이 표현 수단이 단지 취미 생활자들을 위한 것이지 진지한 전문가들을 위한 것은 아니라는 개념이 틀렸음을 입증한다.

(a) has yet to become popular in the art market
(b) is a favored medium of several lesser-known artists
(c) is actually an integral part of a long artistic tradition
(d) has recently lost its popularity among amateur artists

(a) 아직 예술 시장에서 인기를 얻지 못했다
(b) 몇몇 덜 알려진 화가가 선호하는 표현 수단이다
(c) 사실은 오랜 예술 전통의 필수적인 부분이다
(d) 최근에 아마추어 화가들 사이에서 인기를 잃었다

정답 (c)

해설 빈칸에는 수채화에 대한 내용이 와야 한다. 빈칸 앞 문장에서 수채화가 아마추어의 취미로 평판을 받았다(Watercolor painting has acquired a reputation as an amateur pastime.)고 했고, 빈칸 뒤에서 사실 오랜 기간 여러 유명한 화가가 수채화 물감을 작품의 주요 표현 수단으로 사용했다(In fact, many renowned artists, from the Renaissance to modern times, have used watercolor as a major medium for their works, including John Singer Sargent, Edward Hopper, and Georgia O'Keeffe.)고 했으므로, 수채화가 실제로는 오랜 예술 전통의 필수적인 부분이라고 한 (c)가 오면 문맥이 자연스럽게 연결된다.

어휘 watercolor painting col. 수채화 acquire v. 얻다 reputation n. 평판 as prep. ~로(서) amateur adj. 아마추어의 pastime n. 취미 however adv. 하지만 in fact adv. 사실은 renowned adj. 유명한 artist n. 화가 the Renaissance n. 르네상스 modern adj. 현대의 use v. 사용하다 watercolor n. 수채화 물감 major adj. 주요한 medium n. 표현 수단 work n. 작품 include v. 포함하다 prestigious adj. 명망 있는 devote oneself to phr. ~에 전념하다 disprove v. 틀렸음을 입증하다 notion n. 개념 simply adv. 단지 hobbyist n. 취미 생활자 serious adj. 진지한 professional n. 전문가 have yet to do col. 아직 ~하지 않았다 popular adj. 인기 있는 art n. 미술 market n. 시장 favored adj. 선호하는 lesser-known adj. 덜 알려진 actually adv. 실제로는 integral adj. 필수적인 part n. 부분 long adj. 오랜 artistic adj. 예술의 tradition n. 전통 recently adv. 최근에 lose v. 잃다 popularity n. 인기 among prep. ~사이에서

22 빈칸에 들어갈 말 | 문장 일부

난이도 ★★★

Third Culture Kids (TCKs)—children who grow up outside of their home countries because their parents are working or living overseas—generally ---------------------------. Due to this fact, they often think of themselves as belonging to a distinct community, one based on a shared experience of coming of age between distinct national cultures. Unfortunately, even after returning to their home countries, many feel like the only people who truly relate to them are fellow TCKs, as they continue to feel like outsiders not only in foreign countries but also in their countries of origin.

(a) find it easier to relate to each other than to non-TCKs
(b) discover that they adapt easily to unfamiliar cultures
(c) struggle to identify with their parents' generation
(d) grow up to become successful global citizens

부모가 국외에서 일하거나 살아서 고국을 떠나 자라는 아이들인 제3문화 아이들(TCKs)은 일반적으로 제3문화 아이들이 아닌 이들과 공감하기보다 서로 공감하기가 더 쉽다고 생각한다. 이러한 사실 때문에 그들은 종종 자신들이 전혀 다른 공동체에 속한다고 생각하는데, 이 공동체는 전혀 다른 국가 문화 속에서 성장하면서 공유하는 경험에 기반을 둔다. 불행하게도 고국으로 돌아온 후에도 많은 사람들이 자신들과 진정으로 공감하는 사람은 같은 처지에 있는 제3문화 아이들뿐이라고 느끼는데, 이는 그들이 계속 외국뿐만 아니라 출신 국가에서도 외부인처럼 느끼기 때문이다.

(a) 제3문화 아이들이 아닌 이들과 공감하기보다 서로 공감하기가 더 쉽다고 생각한다
(b) 익숙하지 않은 문화에 쉽게 적응한다는 것을 발견한다
(c) 부모 세대와 동질감을 갖는 데 어려움을 겪는다
(d) 자라서 성공적인 세계 시민이 된다

정답 (a)

해설 빈칸에는 제3문화 아이들(TCKs)이 생각하는 내용이 와야 한다. 지문에서 제3문화 아이들(TCKs)의 경우 고국으로 돌아

간 후에도 자신들과 진정으로 공감하는 사람은 같은 처지에 있는 제3문화 아이들뿐이라고 느낀다(Unfortunately, even after returning to their home countries, many feel like the only people who truly relate to them are fellow TCKs)고 했으므로 (a)가 오면 문맥이 자연스럽게 연결된다.

어휘 | Third Culture Kids n. 제3문화 아이들(= TCKs) grow up phr. 자라다 outside of prep. ~의 외부에서 home adj. 고향의 country n. 국가 parent n. 부모 work v. 일하다 live v. 살다 overseas adv. 국외에서 generally adv. 일반적으로 due to prep. ~때문에 fact n. 사실 often adv. 종종 think of A as B phr. A를 B라고 생각하다 belong to phr. ~에 속하다 distinct adj. 전혀 다른 community n. 공동체 based on col. ~에 기반을 두어 shared adj. 공유된 experience n. 경험 come of age idm. 성년이 되다 between prep. ~사이에서 national adj. 국가의 culture n. 문화 unfortunately adv. 불행하게도 even adv. ~도 return v. 돌아오다 feel like phr. ~인 것처럼 느껴지다 only adj. 유일한 truly adv. 진정으로 relate to phr. ~에 공감하다 fellow adj. 같은 처지에 있는 continue to do phr. 계속해서 ~하다 outsider n. 외부인 not only A but also B col. A뿐만 아니라 B도 foreign adj. 외국의 origin n. 출신 find v. ~라고 생각하다 easy adj. 쉬운 discover v. 발견하다 adapt v. 적응하다 easily adv. 쉽게 unfamiliar adj. 익숙하지 않은 struggle v. 어려움을 겪다 identify with phr. ~와 동질감을 갖다 generation n. 세대 become v. ~이 되다 successful adj. 성공적인 global adj. 세계적인 citizen n. 시민

23 빈칸에 들어갈 말 | 문장 일부

난이도 ★★☆

In 1935, US scientists conducted a groundbreaking study on the effect of diet. The scientists fed rats a diet that was very low in calories but that contained all the necessary nutrients for normal development. These rats were then compared with rats that were fed normally. The scientists discovered that ---------------------------. The study has been replicated numerous times with a range of different animal species, with the results showing each time that a low-calorie diet leads to an extended lifespan and a lower risk of contracting diseases. Scientists theorize that limiting calorie intake is beneficial because it slows certain metabolic processes that result in oxidative damage to cells.

(a) normal growth requires sufficient calories and nutrients
(b) the former group lived significantly longer and healthier lives
(c) nutrient deficiencies are the leading cause of abnormal growth
(d) low-calorie diets do not necessarily result in nutrient deficiencies

1935년에 미국 과학자들은 음식의 영향에 관한 획기적인 연구를 수행했다. 과학자들은 쥐에게 칼로리는 매우 낮지만, 정상적인 발달에 필요한 모든 영양소가 들어 있는 음식을 먹였다. 그런 다음 이 쥐들은 정상적으로 먹이를 먹은 쥐와 비교되었다. 과학자들은 전자 그룹이 상당히 더 오래 더 건강하게 살았다는 것을 발견했다. 이 연구는 다양한 동물 종으로 여러 번 반복되었으며, 결과는 매번 저칼로리 음식이 수명을 연장하고 질병에 걸릴 위험을 줄인다는 것을 보여 주었다. 과학자들은 칼로리 섭취를 제한하는 것이 세포에 산화 손상을 일으키는 특정 대사 과정을 늦추기 때문에 유익하다는 이론을 제시했다.

(a) 정상적인 성장에는 충분한 칼로리와 영양소가 필요하다
(b) 전자 그룹이 상당히 더 오래 더 건강하게 살았다
(c) 영양소 결핍은 비정상적인 성장의 주요 원인이다
(d) 저칼로리 음식이 반드시 영양소 결핍을 일으키는 것은 아니다

정답 (b)

해설 | 빈칸에는 과학자들이 발견한 내용이 와야 한다. 빈칸 앞부분에서 칼로리는 매우 낮지만 정상적인 발달에 필요한 모든 영양소가 들어 있는 음식을 먹인 쥐들을 정상적으로 먹이를 먹은 쥐와 비교했다고 했고, 빈칸 뒷부분에서 반복된 연구의 결과는 매번 저칼로리 식단이 수명을 연장하고 질병에 걸릴 위험을 줄인다는 것을 보여 주었다(The study has been replicated numerous times with a range of different animal species, with the results showing each time that a low-calorie diet leads to an extended lifespan and a lower risk of contracting diseases.)고 했으므로, 전자 그룹이 훨씬 더 오래 더 건강하게 살았다고 한 (b)가 오면 문맥이 자연스럽게 연결된다.

어휘 | scientist n. 과학자 conduct v. 수행하다 groundbreaking adj. 획기적인 study n. 연구 effect n. 영향 diet n. 식단 feed v. 먹이

를 주다 **rat** n. 쥐 **calorie** n. 칼로리 **contain** v. ~이 들어 있다 **necessary** adj. 필요한 **nutrient** n. 영양소 **normal** adj. 정상적인 (cf. normally adv. 정상적으로) **development** n. 발달 **then** adv. 그다음에 **compare** v. 비교하다 **discover** v. 발견하다 **replicate** v. 반복하다 **numerous** adj. 수많은 **a range of** col. 유지 **animal** n. 동물 **species** n. 종 **result** n. 결과 **show** v. 보여 주다 **low-calorie** adj. 저칼로리의 **lead to** phr. ~하게 되다 **extended** adj. 늘어난 **lifespan** n. 수명 **risk** n. 위험 **contract** v. 걸리다 **disease** n. 질병 **theorize** v. 이론을 제시하다 **limit** v. 제한하다 **intake** n. 섭취 **beneficial** adj. 유익한 **slow** v. 늦추다 **certain** adj. 특정한 **metabolic** adj. 대사의 **process** n. 과정 **result in** phr. ~을 일으키다 **oxidative** adj. 산화의 **damage** n. 손상 **cell** n. 세포 **growth** n. 성장 **require** v. 필요로 하다 **sufficient** adj. 충분한 **former** adj. 전자의 **group** n. 그룹 **live** v. 살다 **significantly** adv. 상당히 **long** adv. 오래 **healthy** adj. 건강한 **life** n. 삶(pl. lives) **deficiency** n. 결핍 **leading** adj. 주요한 **cause** n. 원인 **abnormal** adj. 비정상적인 **not necessarily** idm. 반드시 ~하는 것은 아니다 **result in** phr. (결과적으로) ~이 되다

24 빈칸에 들어갈 말 | 문장 일부

난이도 ★★★

In the 18th century, the French philosopher and writer Jean-Jacques Rousseau proposed a radically new view of human nature. In contrast to medieval European scholars, who tended to view humans as wicked by nature, Rousseau argued that humans were inherently peaceful and altruistic. According to Rousseau, humans' essential goodness had simply been corrupted by the negative influence of human civilization. This view represented a break with centuries of European religious tradition, which had placed the blame for moral corruption on the effects of original sin. On the basis of his views, Rousseau insisted that it was necessary to --------------------------.

(a) suppress the naturally wicked tendencies of most individuals
(b) modernize the teaching of religion for the betterment of society
(c) reform society in order to preserve the natural goodness of individuals
(d) return to more traditional ways of teaching people about right and wrong

18세기에 프랑스의 철학자이자 작가인 장-자크 루소는 인간 본성에 관해 근본적으로 새로운 견해를 제시했다. 중세 유럽 학자들이 인간을 선천적으로 악한 존재로 보는 경향과는 대조적으로, 루소는 인간이 본질적으로 평화롭고 이타적이라고 주장했다. 루소에 따르면, 인간의 본질적인 선량함은 단지 인간 문명의 부정적인 영향에 의해 타락했을 뿐이다. 이러한 견해는 수세기 동안 이어져 온 유럽의 종교적 전통, 곧 도덕적 타락의 책임을 원죄의 영향으로 돌렸던 전통과 단절됨을 의미했다. 자신의 견해에 근거하여, 루소는 개인의 타고난 선량함을 보존하기 위해 사회를 개혁하는 것이 필요하다고 주장했다.

(a) 대부분의 개인의 선천적으로 악한 경향을 억제하는 것
(b) 사회를 개선하기 위해 종교 교육을 현대화하는 것
(c) 개인의 타고난 선량함을 보존하기 위해 사회를 개혁하는 것
(d) 더 전통적인 방법으로 돌아가 사람들에게 옳고 그름을 가르치는 것

정답 (c)

해설 빈칸에는 루소가 필요하다고 주장한 행동이 와야 한다. 앞부분에서 인간의 본질적인 선량함이 단지 인간 문명의 부정적인 영향에 의해 타락했다고 루소가 주장한 내용이 나왔으므로, 사회를 개혁하여 개인의 타고난 선량함을 보존하는 일이 필요하다고 한 (c)가 오면 문맥이 자연스럽게 연결된다.

어휘 **century** n. 세기 **French** adj. 프랑스의 **philosopher** n. 철학자 **writer** n. 작가 **propose** v. 제안하다 **radically** adv. 근본적으로 **view** n. 견해 **human nature** n. 인간 본성 **in contrast to** idm. ~와 대조적으로 **medieval** adj. 중세의 **European** adj. 유럽의 **scholar** n. 학자 **tend** v. ~하는 경향이 있다 **view A as B** phr. A를 B라고 생각하다 **wicked** adj. 사악한 **by nature** idm. 선천적으로 **argue** v. 주장하다 **inherently** adv. 본질적으로 **peaceful** adj. 평화로운 **altruistic** adj. 이타적인 **according to** prep. ~에 따르면 **essential** adj. 본질적인 **goodness** n. 선량함 **simply** adv. 단지 **corrupt** v. 타락시키다(cf. corruption n. 타락) **negative** adj. 부정적인 **influence** n. 영향 **civilization** n. 문명 **represent** v. 의미하다 **break** n. 단절 **religious** adj. 종교의 **tradition** n. 전통 **placed the blame for A on B** phr. A의 책임을 B에 지우다 **moral** adj. 도덕적인 **effect** n. 영향 **original sin** idm. 원죄 **on the basis of** prep. ~에 근거하여 **insist** v. 주장하다 **necessary** adj. 필요한 **suppress** v. 억제하다 **naturally** adv. 선천적으로 **tendency** n. 경향 **individual** n. 개인 **modernize** v. 현대화하다 **teaching** n. 교육 **religion** n. 종교 **betterment** n. 개선 **society** n. 사회 **reform** v. 개혁하다 **in order to do** idm. ~하기 위해 **preserve** v. 보존하다 **return** v. 돌아가다 **traditional** adj. 전통적인 **way** n. 방식 **teach** v. 가르치다 **right** n. 옳음 **wrong** n. 그름

Which of the following sentences does NOT fit in the overall flow of the passage?

The typical layout of a Japanese office can be seen as a reflection of the traditional values of Japanese society. (a) Unlike American offices, which often feature individual cubicles, Japanese offices tend to have open-plan layouts. (b) Such a layout encourages collaboration, reflecting the Japanese emphasis on collective rather than individual effort. **(c) Nonetheless, Japanese employees who take time off work or come in late are sometimes seen as betraying their coworkers.** (d) At the same time, the open-plan layout facilitates close employee supervision, which is important in Japan's hierarchical society.

다음 중 지문의 전반적인 흐름과 맞지 않는 문장은?

일본 사무실의 전형적인 배치는 일본 사회의 전통적 가치를 반영한 것으로 볼 수 있다. (a) 대개 개별 칸막이 공간을 특징으로 하는 미국의 사무실과는 달리, 일본의 사무실은 개방형으로 배치되는 경향이 있다. (b) 이러한 배치는 협업을 장려하는데, 이는 일본인들이 개인의 노력보다는 집단의 노력을 강조하는 것을 반영한다. **(c) 그럼에도 불구하고, 휴가를 내거나 늦게 출근하는 일본 직원들은 때때로 동료들을 배신하는 것으로 여겨진다.** (d) 동시에 개방형 배치는 일본의 계층 사회에서 중요하게 여겨지는 직원의 면밀한 관리에 용이하다.

정답 (c)

해설 문맥에 어울리지 않는 문장을 고르는 문제이다. 지문의 내용은 일본 사무실의 개방형 배치가 일본 사회의 전통적 가치를 반영하고, 협업을 장려하며, 면밀한 직원 관리에 용이하다는 것이다. (c)는 일본 직원들이 휴가를 내거나 늦게 출근하는 경우에 관한 내용이므로, 지문의 흐름과 맞지 않는다.

어휘 fit v. 꼭 맞다 overall adj. 전반적인 flow n. 흐름 passage n. 지문 typical adj. 전형적인 layout n. 배치 office n. 사무실 reflection n. 반영 traditional adj. 전통적인 value n. 가치 society n. 사회 unlike prep. ~와 달리 often adv. 자주 feature v. 특징으로 하다 individual adj. 개별의 cubicle n. 칸막이한 좁은 장소 tend to do col. ~하는 경향이 있다 open-plan adj. 개방형의 encourage v. 장려하다 collaboration n. 협력 reflect v. 반영하다 emphasis n. 강조 collective adj. 집단의 rather than prep. ~보다는 effort n. 노력 nonetheless adv. 그럼에도 불구하고 employee n. 직원 take time off work col. 휴가를 내다 come in late phr. 늦게 출근하다 sometimes adv. 때때로 see v. 보다 betray v. 배신하다 coworker n. 동료 at the same time adv. 동시에 facilitate v. 용이하게 하다 close adj. 가까운 supervision n. 관리 important adj. 중요한 hierarchical adj. 계층적인

Which of the following sentences does NOT fit in the overall flow of the passage?

A number of factors have contributed to the growing popularity of plastic surgery in recent years. (a) Advancements in medical technology have improved the safety and effectiveness of procedures, in addition to reducing recovery times. (b) On top of that, the growing influence of social media, combined with celebrity culture, has driven many people to pursue perceived beauty standards. (c) Society has also simply become more accepting of plastic surgery, reducing the stigma associated with undergoing procedures purely for aesthetic purposes. **(d) While plastic surgery offers numerous benefits, it is important for anyone contemplating undergoing a cosmetic procedure to have realistic expectations.**

최근 몇 년 동안, 여러 요인이 성형 수술의 인기를 증가시키는 데 이바지했습니다. (a) 의료 기술의 발전은 회복 시간을 줄인 데 더하여 수술의 안전성과 효과를 개선했습니다. (b) 그뿐 아니라 유명 인사 문화와 결합한 소셜 미디어의 영향력 증가는 많은 사람들이 인식된 미의 기준을 추구하게 했습니다. (c) 사회는 또한 성형 수술을 더욱 수용하게 되었고, 이는 순전히 미용 목적으로 수술을 받는 것에 대한 부정적인 인식을 낮췄습니다. **(d) 성형 수술이 많은 이점을 제공하기는 하지만, 성형 수술을 받고자 고려하는 사람은 누구나 현실적인 기대를 하는 것이 중요합니다.**

정답 (d)

해설 문맥에 어울리지 않는 문장을 고르는 문제이다. 주제문인 첫 문장에서 성형 수술의 인기가 증가하는 데 이바지한 여러 요인이 있다고 언급했다. (a), (b), (c)는 그 요인에 해당하는 문장들인데, (d)는 성형 수술을 고려하는 사람들이 현실적인 기대를 해야 한다는 내용으로 문맥에 어울리지 않는다. 따라서 (d)가 정답이다.

어휘 factor n. 요인 contribute v. 이바지하다 growing adj. 증가하는 popularity n. 인기 plastic surgery n. 성형 수술 recent adj. 최근의 advancement n. 발전 medical adj. 의료의 technology n. 기술 improve v. 개선하다 safety n. 안전성 effectiveness n. 효과 procedure n. 수술 in addition to prep. ~에 더하여 reduce v. 줄이다 recovery n. 회복 time n. 시간 on top of idm. ~뿐 아니라 influence n. 영향력 social media n. 소셜 미디어 combine v. 결합하다 celebrity n. 유명 인사 culture n. 문화 drive A to do v. A가 ~하도록 만들다 pursue v. 추구하다 perceive v. 인식하다 beauty n. 미 standard n. 기준 society n. 사회 simply adv. 단순히 accept v. 받아들이다 stigma n. 부정적인 인식 associate v. 연관시키다 undergo v. 받다 purely adv. 순전히 aesthetic adj. 미적인 purpose n. 목적 while conj. ~이긴 하지만 offer v. 제공하다 numerous adj. 많은 benefit n. 이점 important adj. 중요한 contemplate v. 고려하다 cosmetic adj. 성형의 realistic adj. 현실적인 expectation n. 기대

27-28   1지문 2문항

Read the following passage and answer the questions.

[27]In 1972, sociologist Stanley Cohen introduced the concept of moral panics. He defined these events as widespread outbreaks of fear, anger, or outrage stemming from the perception that some specific behavior, group, or phenomenon poses a significant threat to the well-being of society. [28]Some moral panics arise from actual threats, while others arise from purely imaginary ones. Regardless of whether the threat is real or imaginary, the extent of the danger to society is grossly exaggerated by the people caught up in the moral panic. Since Cohen's time, the concept of moral panics has been used to explain a number of significant historical events. For example, the McCarthy era in the United States has been characterized as a moral panic. During this period, from the late 1940s to the mid-1950s, US senator Joseph McCarthy whipped up public hysteria about the supposed influence of communism and Soviet agents on American institutions. As a result of the panic, thousands of innocent Americans were investigated by the Federal Bureau of Investigation (FBI) and blacklisted from participating in the entertainment industry. Another example is the War on Drugs, which reached its peak in the 1990s. During this period of US history, society became obsessed with the supposed threat of drugs. Due to these exaggerated fears, harsh laws were passed, resulting in many people being handed long prison sentences for relatively minor offenses.

다음 지문을 읽고 질문에 답하시오.

[27]1972년에 사회학자 스탠리 코언은 도덕적 공황이라는 개념을 소개했다. 그는 이러한 사건들을 특정 행동, 그룹, 또는 현상이 사회의 안정에 중대한 위협을 가한다는 인식에서 비롯되어 널리 퍼진 공포, 분노, 또는 격분의 발현으로 정의했다. [28]어떤 도덕적 공황은 실제의 위협에서 발생하는 반면에, 다른 도덕적 공황은 순전히 상상 속 위협에서 발생한다. 위협이 실제인지 상상인지와 관계없이, 사회에 대한 위험의 범위는 도덕적 공황에 휩쓸린 사람들에 의해 크게 과장된다. 코언의 시대 이후로 도덕적 공황의 개념은 여러 중요한 역사적 사건을 설명하는 데 사용되었다. 예를 들어, 미국의 매카시 시대는 도덕적 공황으로 특징지어졌다. 1940년대 후반부터 1950년대 중반까지의 기간에 미국 상원의원 조지프 매카시는 공산주의와 소련 요원들이 미국 기관에 미치리라 추정되는 영향으로 대중의 히스테리를 선동했다. 공황의 결과로, 수천 명의 무고한 미국인이 연방 수사국(FBI)의 조사를 받았고, 엔터테인먼트 산업에 참여하는 것으로 블랙리스트에 올랐다. 또 다른 예는 마약 전쟁으로, 1990년대에 정점에 이르렀다. 미국 역사에서 이 기간 동안 사회는 마약의 추정되는 위협에 집착하게 되었다. 이러한 과장된 두려움 때문에, 엄격한 법률이 통과되어 많은 사람이 비교적 사소한 범죄로 장기간의 징역형을 선고받았다.

어휘 sociologist n. 사회학자 introduce v. 소개하다 concept n. 개념 moral adj. 도덕적인 panic n. 공황 define v. 정의하다 event n. 사건 widespread adj. 널리 퍼진 outbreak n. 발발 fear n. 두려움 anger n. 분노 outrage n. 격분 stem from phr. ~에서 비롯되다 perception n. 인식 specific adj. 특정한 behavior n. 행동 group n. 그룹 phenomenon n. 현상 pose v. 제기하다 significant adj. 중요한 threat n. 위협 well-being n. 복지, 안정 society n. 사회 arise v. 발생하다 actual adj. 실제의 while conj. ~인 데 반하여 purely adv. 순전히 imaginary adj. 상상의 regardless of prep. ~에 상관없이 whether conj. ~인지 여부 real adj. 실제의 extent

n. 범위 **danger** n. 위험 **grossly** adv. 크게 **exaggerate** v. 과장하다 **caught up in** idm. ~에 휩쓸린 **since** prep. ~이후로 **explain** v. 설명하다 **significant** adj. 중요한 **historical** adj. 역사적인 **for example** phr. 예를 들어 **era** n. 시대 **characterize** v. 특징짓다 **period** n. 기간 **senator** n. 상원의원 **whip up** phr. 선동하다 **public** n. 대중 **hysteria** n. 히스테리 **supposed** adj. 추정되는 **influence** n. 영향 **communism** n. 공산주의 **agent** n. 요원 **institution** n. 기관 **as a result of** phr. ~의 결과로 **innocent** adj. 무죄의 **investigate** v. 조사하다 **Federal Bureau of Investigation** n. 연방수사국(= FBI) **blacklist** v. 블랙리스트에 올리다 **participate** v. 참여하다 **entertainment** n. 엔터테인먼트 **industry** n. 산업 **example** n. 예 **war** n. 전쟁 **drug** n. 마약 **reach** v. 도달하다 **peak** n. 정점 **history** n. 역사 **become** v. ~가 되다 **obsessed** adj. 집착하는 **due to** prep. ~때문에 **harsh** adj. 가혹한 **law** n. 법 **pass** v. 통과시키다 **result in** phr. (결과적으로) ~이 되다 **hand** v. 건네주다 **prison sentence** n. 징역형 **relatively** adv. 상대적으로, 비교적으로 **minor** adj. 사소한 **offense** n. 범죄

27 글의 목적, 주제, 요지, 제목 | 주제
난이도 ★★★

What is the best title for the passage?

(a) The Concept of Moral Panics: Definition and Examples
(b) Updating the Definition of Moral Panics: Latest Discoveries
(c) Moral Panics: How They Have Changed throughout History
(d) The Effects of Moral Panics: Examples from around the World

지문에 가장 알맞은 제목은?

(a) 도덕적 공황의 개념: 정의와 예시
(b) 도덕적 공황의 정의 업데이트: 최신 발견
(c) 도덕적 공황: 역사 속에서 어떻게 변했는가
(d) 도덕적 공황의 영향: 전 세계의 예시

정답 (a)

해설 지문은 도덕적 공황의 개념을 소개하고, 여러 역사적 사건을 예로 들어 이를 설명하고 있다. 따라서 (a)가 가장 적절한 제목이다.

Paraphrasing The Concept of Moral Panics: Definition and Examples
→ The concept of moral panics and its examples

어휘 **title** n. 제목 **passage** n. 지문 **definition** n. 정의 **example** n. 예시 **update** v. 업데이트하다 **latest** adj. 최신의 **discovery** n. 발견 **change** v. 변하다 **throughout** prep. ~을 통해 **history** n. 역사 **effect** n. 영향

28 글의 내용과 일치하는 것 | 일치
난이도 ★★★

Which of the following is correct according to the passage?

(a) Cohen expanded upon the existing theory of moral panics in 1972.
(b) **Moral panics arise in response to both imaginary and real dangers.**
(c) McCarthy warned the public about threats to communism.
(d) The US War on Drugs reached its highest point before 1990.

다음 중 지문의 내용과 일치하는 것은?

(a) 코언은 1972년에 기존의 도덕적 공황 이론을 확장했다.
(b) **도덕적 공황은 상상과 실제 위험 모두에 대한 반응으로 발생한다.**
(c) 매카시는 공산주의가 받는 위협에 대해 대중에게 경고했다.
(d) 미국의 마약 전쟁은 1990년 이전에 정점에 이르렀다.

정답 (b)

해설 지문의 내용과 일치하는 것을 찾는 문제이다. 지문에서, 어떤 도덕적 공황은 실제의 위협에서 발생하는 반면에, 다른 도덕적 공황은 순전히 상상 속 위협에서 발생한다(Some moral panics arise from actual threats, while others arise from purely imaginary ones.)고 했다. 따라서 이를 바꿔서 표현한 (b)가 정답이다.

Paraphrasing Some moral panics arise from actual threats, while others arise from purely imaginary ones.
→ Moral panics arise in response to both imaginary and real dangers

29-30   1지문 2문항

Read the following passage and answer the questions.

²⁹*The Playboy of the Western World*, a three-act play by Irish playwright J. M. Synge, presented a strikingly original portrayal of the common people of Ireland. ³⁰The play premiered in 1907 at Dublin's Abbey Theater, the national theater and one of Ireland's leading cultural institutions. At the time, Ireland remained firmly under control of the English, who had tended to depict the Irish as boorish subordinates. In opposition to these unflattering portraits, Irish nationalist writers had depicted poor Irish characters in often highly romantic terms, transforming these characters into symbols of national pride. Synge, who was fiercely nationalistic himself, saw the danger of such portraits, arguing that they were just as misrepresentative of the actual people as the insulting depictions by English writers. He wanted to present a true-to-life portrait, so instead of showing characters valiantly suffering under the burden of poverty, he depicted them often reveling in the crude humor and cheerful immorality of their surroundings. Unsurprisingly, his play was attacked by many of his own people, with the audience at the premiere going so far as to riot.

다음 지문을 읽고 질문에 답하시오.

²⁹<서쪽 나라의 멋쟁이>는 아일랜드의 극작가 J. M. 싱이 쓴 3막극으로, 아일랜드의 보통 사람들을 상당히 독창적으로 묘사했다. ³⁰이 연극은 1907년 아일랜드의 국립 극장이자 주요 문화 기관 중 하나인 더블린의 애비 극장에서 초연되었다. 당시 아일랜드는 확고하게 영국의 지배 아래 있었는데, 영국인은 아일랜드인을 천한 부하로 묘사하는 경향이 있었다. 이러한 호의적이지 않은 묘사에 반대하여, 아일랜드 민족주의 작가들은 가난한 아일랜드 캐릭터를 종종 매우 낭만적인 용어로 묘사하며, 이 캐릭터들을 민족적 자부심의 상징으로 변모시켰다. 스스로도 맹렬한 민족주의자였던 싱은 이러한 묘사의 위험성을 깨달았으며, 이것들이 영국 작가들에 의한 모욕적인 묘사만큼이나 실제의 사람들을 왜곡한다고 주장했다. 그는 사실적으로 묘사하고 싶었기 때문에, 캐릭터들이 가난한 짐을 지고 용감하게 받아들이는 모습을 보여 주는 대신, 그들이 주변의 거친 유머와 쾌활한 부도덕을 한껏 즐기는 모습을 묘사했다. 아니나 다를까 그의 연극은 자기 동포들에게서 공격을 많이 받았으며, 초연의 관객들은 심지어 폭동까지 일으켰다.

어휘   passage n. 지문 playboy n. 한량 western world col. 서양 act n. (연극 등의) 막 play n. 연극 Irish adj. 아일랜드의 playwright n. 극작가 present v. 묘사하다 strikingly adv. 눈에 띄게 original adj. 독창적인 portrayal n. 묘사 common adj. 일반적인 premiere v. 초연하다; n. 초연 theater n. 극장 national adj. 국가의 leading adj. 주요한 cultural adj. 문화의 institution n. 기관 remain v. 남다 firmly adv. 확고하게 under control of idm. ~의 지배 아래 tend to do col. ~하는 경향이 있다 depict v. 묘사하다 as prep. ~로서 boorish adj. 천박한 subordinate n. 하급자 in opposition to idm. ~에 반대하여 unflattering adj. 호의적이지 않은 portrait n. 묘사 nationalist adj. 민족주의의 writer n. 작가 poor adj. 가난한 character n. 캐릭터 often adv. 자주 highly adv. 매우 romantic adj. 로맨틱한 term n. 용어 transform v. 변형시키다 symbol n. 상징 national adj. 민족의 pride n. 자부심 fiercely adv. 맹렬하게 nationalistic adj. 민족주의적인 see v. 보다 danger n. 위험 argue v. 주장하다 just as A as B idm. B만큼 A한 as prep. ~만큼, ~처럼 misrepresentative adj. 왜곡된 actual adj. 실제의 insulting adj. 모욕적인 depiction n. 묘사 true-to-life adj. 사실적인 so conj. 그래서 instead of prep. ~대신에 show v. 보여 주다 valiantly adv. 용감하게 suffer v. 고통받다 burden n. 부담, 짐 poverty n. 빈곤 revel v. 한껏 즐기다 crude adj. 거친 humor n. 유머 cheerful adj. 쾌활한 immorality n. 부도덕 surrounding n. 주변 unsurprisingly adv. 아니나 다를까 attack v. 공격하다 own adj. 자신의 audience n. 관객 go so far as to do idm. 심지어 ~하기까지 하다 riot v. 폭동을 일으키다

29   글의 목적, 주제, 요지, 제목 | 주제   난이도 ★★★

What is the main idea of the passage?

(a) Synge's uncommonly realistic depiction of Irish people caused controversy.
(b) Synge promoted nationalism in response to English depictions of the Irish.

지문의 주제는 무엇인가?

(a) 싱의 극도로 현실적인 아일랜드인 묘사가 논란을 일으켰다.
(b) 싱은 영국인들이 아일랜드인을 묘사한 것에 대응하여 민족주의를 고취했다.
(c) 싱은 영국 작가들의 부정확한 아일랜드인 묘

(c) Synge was critical of inaccurate depiction of the Irish by English authors.
(d) Synge's blend of nationalism and romanticism divided Irish audiences.

사에 비판적이었다.
(d) 싱의 민족주의와 낭만주의의 혼합이 아일랜드 관객들을 분열시켰다.

정답 (a)

해설 지문의 주제를 묻는 문제이다. 지문 전체에서 Synge이 아일랜드인들을 현실적으로 묘사한 것이 어떤 반응을 불러일으켰는지를 설명하고 있다. 따라서 (a)가 정답이다. (b)는 Synge이 민족주의를 고취했다고 하는데, 지문에서는 그가 민족주의자였다고만 언급한다. (c)는 영국 작가의 부정확한 묘사에 비판적이었다고 하는데, 지문에서는 영국 작가들뿐만 아니라 아일랜드 민족주의 작가들에 대해서도 비판적이었다고 언급한다. (d)는 민족주의와 낭만주의의 혼합이라고 하는데, 지문에서는 Synge이 낭만주의적인 묘사를 피하고 현실적으로 묘사하려 했다고 언급한다.

Paraphrasing strikingly original portrayal → uncommonly realistic depiction

어휘 uncommonly adv. 극도로 realistic adj. 현실적인 cause v. ~을 일으키다 controversy n. 논란 promote v. 고취하다 nationalism n. 국민주의 in response to prep. ~에 대응하여, ~에 반응하여 depiction n. 묘사 critical adj. 비판적인 inaccurate adj. 부정확한 author n. 작가 blend n. 혼합 romanticism n. 낭만주의 divide v. 분열시키다 audience n. 관객

30 글의 내용과 일치하는 것 | 일치

난이도 ★★★

Which of the following is correct according to the passage?

(a) The play was initially performed at a highly reputable theater.
(b) Synge wrote the play following Ireland's independence from England.
(c) Irish nationalist writers tended to avoid depicting lower-class Irish characters.
(d) Synge's play was celebrated upon its premiere but subsequently attracted harsh criticism.

다음 중 지문의 내용과 일치하는 것은 무엇인가?

(a) 연극은 처음에 매우 명성이 있는 극장에서 공연되었다.
(b) 싱은 아일랜드가 영국으로부터 독립한 후에 연극을 썼다.
(c) 아일랜드 민족주의 작가들은 하층 계급의 아일랜드 캐릭터를 묘사하는 것을 피했다.
(d) 싱의 연극은 초연 때 찬양받았지만 이후에는 엄중한 비판을 불러일으켰다.

정답 (a)

해설 지문의 내용과 일치하는 것을 묻는 문제이다. 지문에 따르면, 연극은 아일랜드의 국립 극장이자 주요 문화 기관 중 하나인 더블린의 애비 극장에서 초연되었다(The play premiered in 1907 at Dublin's Abbey Theater, the national theater and one of Ireland's leading cultural institutions.). 이를 바꿔 표현한 (a)가 정답이다.

Paraphrasing The play premiered in 1907 at Dublin's Abbey Theater, the national theater and one of Ireland's leading cultural institutions.
→ The play was initially performed at a highly reputable theater.

어휘 initially adv. 처음에 perform v. 공연하다 highly adv. 매우 reputable adj. 명성이 있는 write v. 쓰다 following prep. ~ 다음에 independence n. 독립 avoid v. 피하다 lower-class adj. 하층 계급의 celebrate v. 찬양하다 subsequently adv. 이후에 attract v. 불러일으키다 harsh adj. 엄중한 criticism n. 비판

IM-TEPS

Intermediate Test of English Proficiency developed by
Seoul National University

IM-TEPS 기출유형문제집 1회분

발행일   2024년 7월 31일

지은이   에듀팡 어학연구소 편집·해설

펴낸이   애듀팡 출판팀

펴낸곳   에듀팡

주소   서울특별시 구로구 디지털로 306 대륭포스트타워 2차 612호

홈페이지 www.edupang.com

고객센터 1644-1777

출판등록 2024년 7월 11일 제25100-2024-000041호

ISBN   979-11-988484-1-3 53740

MEMO